NEW AGE P

A portable palmistry workshop

NEW AGE PALMISTRY

A portable palmistry workshop

PETER HAZEL

LOTHIAN PUBLISHING COMPANY PTY LTD
MELBOURNE SYDNEY AUCKLAND

for Margaretha,
for all the love and patience . . .

A Lothian book

LOTHIAN PUBLISHING COMPANY PTY LTD
11 Munro Street, Port Melbourne, Victoria 3207

Copyright © Peter Hazel 1989
First published 1989

National Library of Australia
Cataloguing-in-publication data:

Hazel, Peter, 1947–
    New age palmistry, a portable palmistry workshop.
    ISBN 0 85091 377 2.
    1. Palmistry. I. Title.
133.6

Designed by Jane Pennells & Jo Waite
Typeset in Sabon and Copperplate Gothic by Bookset,
    Melbourne
Printed by The Book Printer, Melbourne

PREFACE

*'Palmistry has long been considered a mystic art,
when in fact it is a valuable and precise method of
qualifying and quantifying all aspects of human
potential.'*

— Peter West

*'Lines have not been traced without cause in the
hands of men. They evidently emanate from the
influence of heaven and from human
individuality.'*

— Aristotle

This book came into being during a period
when I was tempted by the vanity of teaching
and, in the autumn of 1987, taught a six-
month course in Medical Palmistry at the
South Australian College of Botanic Medicine
and Natural Therapies run by Marni
Morrow, herbalist and naturopath.

There was a class of 12, several of
whom were 4th year students of Naturopathy;
the remainder were interested adults. They
were a formidably bright group, hungry for
knowledge and good information.

The main problem for me as a teacher
was to supply the students with a suitable
text. I wanted to present them with an organised body of knowledge in some easily access-
ible form. This proved impossible to find,
however.

My own knowledge was acquired
slowly. Having no teacher, I relied on books,
beginning with Katherine St Hill and Cheiro,
both famous palmists around the turn of the
century. These writers were very keen on
gloomy, moralistic interpretations. They had
a good grasp of the traditional stream of

palmistry, but this was coloured by the particular social mores and crude psychological knowledge of their day. It takes a keen student to wade through all the Victorian prose, and the jumbled, poorly organised mass of detail.

Adhering strictly to traditional nomenclature, I sorted Victorian value judgements from the data, and proceeded to create New Age views. Some definitions were arrived at only after lengthy discussion with students and other practitioners. The result is the book you now hold in your hands. *New Age Palmistry* is a technical manual, designed for ease of use, to provide instant access to an ancient art for both the experienced palmist and the novice.

Peter Hazel
Adelaide

Contents

INTRODUCTION

Palmistry is based on the belief that each part of the body reflects the state — both physical and mental — of the entire organism. When one is ill, there are many obvious physical signals. Your hair, skin and colouring are all affected. Your body is an ecosystem, and everything in it is related and connected to everything else.

The palm and the iris are special in that they reflect the state of the entire organism.

Consider your hand; with its 27 fine bones and intricate network of sinew and muscle it is the most complex biological tool ever evolved. Its versatility is astonishing. It can lay bricks, sew point, make love, kill, and wriggle in all directions at once. Just imagine life without your hands; how impossible it would be to get along without them. We use them to communicate when we speak and when we are silent. It is hands that carry guns and that change nappies. Aristotle called the hand 'the organ of organs, the active agent of the passive powers of the entire system'.

It would be difficult to imagine how human civilisation could have developed without hands to build. The hand is so full of information that even a handshake will tell you a great deal about a person. The hands also form one pole of our intricate nervous system (the feet are the other pole). Between them the feet and hands contain more than one third of the body's surface nerve receptors, and both are rich in reflex points.

The palm is criss-crossed with lines: three major lines — the Life, Head and Heart lines — plus a variety of minor lines that appear on the hands of all physically and mentally normal people. However, variations in length, thickness, colour and regularity are infinite. Each of us has a unique hand, different to anybody else's. This is due to the fact that the lines are caused by the differences and experiences that make us individual.

It would be impossible to estimate the age of the science and art of palmistry. There exist fragments of literature on palmistry from the Aryan age, some 6000 years ago. Ancient Vedic literature from India contains many volumes on the subject. So it would appear that palmistry has existed as an established art for a very long time. It probably took many generations of careful observation to hone palmistry to its current precise form. Folk knowledge passed down verbally is a legitimate stream of human learning. Folk knowledge, in which we can include herbalism, shamanism in all its varieties and even astronomy, is highly refined and useful information. This knowledge was hard-won: we know some mushrooms are deadly probably because long ago someone died after eating them. Folk knowledge is not rigid, however: it is added to and expanded by succeeding generations as social values change, and information no longer relevant is discarded.

Palmistry was also practised in Greece where, in 423 BC, Anaxagoras remarked that palmistry was 'a study worthy of an enquiring and educated mind'. It remained a worthy *study until the advent of the Dark Age in Europe, a period when religious fanaticism was at a peak, with alert clergy and pious laymen forever on the lookout for heresy. The history of Christianity at this time is a story of the suppression of knowledge. Palmistry, along with wicca, astronomy and herbalism, was brutally suppressed and its practitioners condemned, with the consequence that the art moved underground. Further reference to palmistry is not found until 1440.*

During this 'dark' period, palmistry became the province of gypsies, whose skills were not very profound, usually woven about cheerful fortunes that would ensure good tips.

There was something of a revival in the 19th century, when the new scientific age brought forth men who tried to put palmistry on a scientific footing. Foremost among these are the Frenchmen D'Arpigny and Desbarolles, who systematically studied the hand, creating classifications used by some palmists today. Regrettably, however, official recognition of the science is as far off today as it ever was. Though there exists, as any doctor would agree, a huge number of mysteries regarding the human body and the way it functions, palmistry has been rejected by physicians and academics without much investigation.

This folk knowledge has survived despite all opposition, however, and interest in it blossoms today. Palmistry, like naturopathy, herbalism and astrology, may one day be fully accepted.

That the palm is a mirror of the human self is a gift of nature.

How to Use this Book

This portable palmistry workshop is designed to provide instant access to an ancient art. It consists of two parts: the **Notes** and the **Workshop**.

The Notes are located at the back of the book and provide vital information necessary for the serious student of palmistry, as well as the interested layperson. They tell you what to look for on the lines and the mounts, how to judge time, and list some of the many possible uses of palmistry.

If you wish, you may leave the Notes for later study, and proceed directly to the Workshop.

The Workshop consists of a series of questions and answers that will take you methodically through a palm reading. To conduct a read — of your own hand, or of a willing subject — simply work your way through the Workshop.

Each question requires a yes or no answer. When the answer is yes, the accompanying description applies to the subject. If the answer is no, simply pass on to the next question.

These questions systematically examine the various aspects of the hand, beginning with broad outlines and continuing to explore the finer details, covering the lines and mounts, and the marks on the fingers. Much of the material has come from original research, and has not appeared in print before.

You may complete the reading having received only a few or a great many yes answers. This reflects the simplicity or complexity of the subject. You may find contradictions; these can often represent conflict and contradiction within the subject.

Do not *take any single definition as final. The golden rule of palmistry states that no one aspect should be considered in isolation. It is your task to weave the various definitions into a holistic picture of the subject (see note on* Interpretation and Intuition*).*

Always read the right hand (see note on Left and right hands*).*

Your first few readings may seem slow, even difficult, but regular use of this portable palmistry workshop will lead to familiarity and expertise.

THE WORKSHOP

*The **Workshop** is designed to lead the novice through a reading. It consists of 232 questions with answers, which cover most aspects of a read.*

Each question requires a yes *or* no *answer. If the answer is* yes, *the accompanying definition applies to the subject. If the answer is* no, *simply pass on to the next question.*

As you become familiar with this system, your need to refer to it will decrease. Laid out according to traditional classifications, e.g. in lines and mounts, it is an easy to use reference.

THE HAND

The hand shows the broad outlines of a person's character. The first step is to ascertain the *hand type*. There are four main types. To do this, measure the palm and determine whether it is a short or a long palm.

WIDTH OF PALM

A *short* palm is square, or wider than it is long.

A *long* palm is longer than it is wide.

Now determine whether the fingers are short or long. To do this, measure the palm and fingers as shown below.

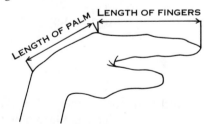

LENGTH OF PALM LENGTH OF FINGERS

Short fingers are equal to or shorter than the palm.

Long fingers are longer than the palm.

Has the hand

A long palm with long fingers (Water hand)?

This is also called the Sensitive Hand and is feminine positive. It is the hand of a sensitive, sympathetic, cautious, reserved, intuitive and psychic person with emotion-based reasoning and a rich inner life. Concern for taste and appearance, and quality of lifestyle and re-lationships are characteristic of this person-ality, as is a caring nature and a sense of justice.

These people tend to be procrastinating and overly self-critical, however. In need of constant encouragement and support, they may lack confidence, wilting easily in the face of criticism and opposition.

Sex life: sentimental and romantic, they are easily ruled by love, and need harmony and safe comfortable surroundings.

A long palm with short fingers (Fire hand)?

This is also called the Instinctive Hand and is feminine negative. It signals an artistic, changeable, passionate and creative person-ality; an adventurous risk-taker. These people are non-authoritarian, highly motivated, extroverted, emotional, excitable and prone to sudden enthusiasm. They are overly emo-tional, and can be selfish, aggressive and demanding.

Sex life: impulsive and easily bored by routine, they need intensity and/or variety, and are usually sentimental and romantic.

A short palm with long fingers (Air hand)?

This is known as the Intellectual Hand and is masculine negative. The sign of a clever, inter-ested personality, with a curious mind and a love of study. This person is intellectual in outlook, very analytical, systematic and conceptualising, and in possession of good communications skills. Reason tends to rule the emotions of such people, who often fear the irrational pressures of emotions. They can be cool and unsympathetic, impatient with routine, restless, feel the need to be fully interested in whatever they are doing.

Sex life: A love of adventure and novelty; dislike of routine relationships.

A short palm with short fingers (Earth hand)?

This is also known as the Practical Hand and is masculine positive. It is the hand of a practical, conventional, reliable personality; solid, strict, strong and productive.

He or she is likely to be authoritarian in outlook, with a love of order, routine and systems, and dislike of uncertainty and change. Cautious and single-minded, the person with this shape of hand tends to need material security, and is prone to temper attacks when stressed.

Sex life: a need for security and regularity dominates; they are non-adventurous, preferring routine to change.

Now feel the subject's hand all over. Is the hand

Very soft and spongy to the touch?

This denotes sensuality and self-interest. One who delights in eating, drinking and sexual pleasure, but who is prone to obesity, and in danger of over-indulgence, addiction and dependency.

It also shows a dislike of drudgery, routine, discomfort and privation. People with this type of hand are usually very friendly, generous and gregarious.

Quite flexible — the fingers bend backwards easily?

This indicates the flexible nature of one with many interests and hobbies, who may be multi-talented. The sign of a versatile and adaptable person, with good coping skills, who enjoys and seeks change and novelty.

However, restlessness and an inability to settle down may also be a trait of the person with this type of hand. This may give rise to the 'jack of all trades, master of none' type.

Hard, stiff and unyielding?

This shows an unyielding personality, resolute and determined, who may be stubborn and finds it very difficult to compromise. Poor diplomatic skills and tactlessness are also indicated, along with fixed attitudes and difficulty in coping with change.

This hand often belongs to one who is active and physical.

Firm, yet quite elastic?

The mark of a balanced type, adaptable to changing life and work situations, with a positive, optimistic outlook.

Such people are self-reliant and usually able to enjoy life.

Very smooth?

This suggests a creative personality, very impulsive, versatile and adaptable; one who may be poetic, romantic and imaginative. In a badly aspected hand it can indicate dishonesty, exaggeration and posing, and a lack of attention to detail.

Very bony or knobby?

This is sometimes called the 'philosophical' hand and indicates the intellectual outlook of one given to reflection and a liking for order and system.

The negative aspects of this feature are dogmatic viewpoints, fault-finding with anyone who does not agree, and tactlessness. The subject may also be prone to worry and tension.

Hard and thin?

This can be the hand of one with delicate health. Psychologically, it shows a cool, even cold nature, and selfishness, resulting in an inability to see another's point of view and an unsympathetic nature motivated by self-interest.

Distinctly hollow in the middle of the palm?

This betrays a negative self-image and poor self-esteem resulting in timidity, shyness, and a lack of self-confidence.

The subject with this feature may be prone to worry and pessimism, and possibly lacks self-knowledge.

Note the colouring. Is the hand

Pale, colourless, dead white?

This is the hand of an emotionally cool person, a withdrawn, selfish and egocentric person. This may also indicate a lack of physical energy.

Pinkish, possibly mottled with white?

This is the normal colour of basic good health, and shows a tendency to buoyant animal spirits.

Red, or with large red patches?

This shows vitality and high energy, vigour and sensuality. If very red, it is a sign of a tendency to aggression and violence. In women, it is a possible indication of pregnancy or a hormone imbalance.

Compare the hand size to the overall physique of the subject. Are the hands

Proportionally large?

This signals a talent for detail and minutiae, with a capability for fine and delicate work, possibly in crafts and arts. These people enjoy detailed, drawn-out analysis of relationships and situations.

Proportionally small?

This is a sign of one who is capable of grasping ideas as a whole, though not in fine detail; a person who is likely to see the overview, but is often unable to come to grips with the components of a situation.

Such personalities often have an inability to judge personal limits, leading to dreaming, excitability and fantasising. They often harbour large-scale hopes and plans, which usually fail due to lack of attention to detail.

Examine the number of lines visible in the palm. Is the palm

Covered with many lines (full or crowded hand)?

This is called the 'full' or 'crowded' hand and often belongs to a highly strung individual with a vivid imagination, perceptive and often over-sensitive. The crowded hand can also indicate creativity, unpredictability and excitability. These people are often good at organising and delegating, but are themselves fairly

impractical. They are disciplinarians, yet poor at self-discipline. The many lines actually represent an abundance of energy that is, however, very scattered and poorly directed.

Marked with a moderate number of clear lines (moderate hand)?

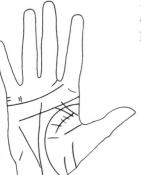

Indicates a good balance between enthusiasm and indifference; a tendency toward practicality.

Marked with only a few, basic lines (empty hand)?

The meaning of this varies with each hand type. In a sensitive Water or Fire hand, it can be a sign of deep spirituality, and the mark of a self-assured person. Indian palmistry calls it the mark of an 'old soul'.

In more elementary hands (Earth or Air), it shows a no-nonsense, straightforward, unoriginal and insensitive character; one well-suited to service, who is conventional, obedient, punctual and orderly. Though often slow, they are nevertheless thorough.

In relation to the palm, are the fingers

Longer?

> Denotes a sensitive, artistic nature, and a love of detail; possibly spiritually inclined, but with an element of pride that can lead to intolerance.

Shorter?

> Shows a concise, precise person, quick to make judgement; one who can see things as a whole, but is troubled or intimidated by detail.

About equal in length?

> Represents a balance between long and short fingers; honesty.

Now, examine the fingertips. Are they

Round?

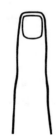

> This is the 'ordinary' shape and represents a strong-minded intellectual person whose actions are based in both reason and emotion.

Square?

> A sign of practicality and craftsmanship; a physically strong person whose actions are based on reason.

Spatulate?

This shows a practical, capable person; a good instigator and organiser.

Pointed?

A person who acts mainly through intuition and emotion. These are traditionally described as 'psychic' fingers.

Does the little finger curve inwards?

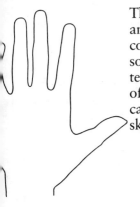

This is often called the 'wilt of self-sacrifice' and indicates a self-effacing, compromising, compliant, 'anything-for-peace' type of person. It can also indicate a masochistic character and may even represent sexual difficulties of some sort. In a very well-aspected hand, it can represent business ability and financial skill.

THE THUMB

The thumb represents the ego, and shows characteristics of self-confidence, stubbornness, logical ability, will-power and determination.

First you must determine whether the subject has a *long* or *short* thumb. To do this, lay the thumb alongside the edge of the hand.

If the thumb reaches halfway along the bottom phlange of the index finger, it is *long*.

If it does not reach halfway along this phlange, it is *short*.

Is the thumb

Long?

This shows a strong character with developed sense of duty, intellectual strength and an active ego. People with these thumbs tend to be ruled by emotion in a dogmatic way; they are very practical people, able to put ideas into action, and transform dreams into reality. It also indicates ambition and strong will.

Short?

This indicates weak will, poor logical powers, and little ambition. People with these thumbs are generally ruled by emotional considerations, and are likely to have close family ties due to a sense of insecurity.

They are often indecisive, given to procrastination, and lack personal energy and power. They may also be bad-tempered, and capable of bursts of passionate self-righteous anger.

Quite stiff, inflexible and unyielding?

This signifies an inflexible, dogmatic, stubborn and probably tactless individual with a rigid personality and poor coping skills. This person may well be self-absorbed and unable to see another's point of view.

This thumb is the mark of an unimaginative, unsympathetic character who must 'have his or her own way'.

Rather supple and flexible?

This shows a charming, graceful character, very tactful and a convincing flatterer. The flexible thumb indicates a very flexible ego, capable of compromise and sympathy to others' viewpoints.

People with this type of thumb are usually accommodating and cope with life skilfully.

Does it

Curve backward at the tip?

Yes: This indicates a talent for living. One that is extravagant, adaptable, quick to learn, and often in possession of a contented nature. The person with this thumb has considerable will-power, modified by genuine concern for others, and is a skilled and convincing liar if the occasion demands.

No: This marks a very practical, stiff-necked, stubborn character. One that is terminally determined, yet usually very cautious, secretive and self-controlled.

Is the thumb

Set low on the hand, near the wrist?

This suggests a creative, generous and extravagant nature; a gregarious and sociable nature, hospitable and outgoing.

It also shows an ego deeply rooted in emotion, of one who acts and reasons through the feelings rather than logic.

Set high on the hand, near the fingers?

This is the mark of a very cautious nature, with a tendency to conservatism, and often stubborn.

The person with this thumb has a very intellectual outlook, with most actions and relationships governed by logic rather than feeling.

Now study the hand in a relaxed attitude, noting the angle that the thumb juts from the hand.

Is this angle

Narrow (less than 30 degrees)?

Indicates a withdrawn, timid ego, capable of limited response, low drive, and little ambition. It shows a person with limited perception, due to self-absorption, who is motivated mainly by self-interest.

Wide (more than 30 degrees)?

The wider the angle, the more pronounced the characteristics of discipline, will-power, and sense of direction. This is a sign of an extrovert, one who is courageous and has leadership qualities.

Note the shape of the tip. Is it

Pointed?

An intuitive, frivolous, and possibly superstitious person.

Square?

Shows a stubborn, practical, sagacious and loyal person.

Round?

Indicates a balance between logic and emotion.

Clubbed?

The sign of a bad-tempered, violent nature. Traditionally called the 'murderer's thumb'.

Flat and thin?

People with subtle, quick minds, but low physical energy. They often fail to finish what they start.

Broad and thick?

A materialist; sensual, with a love of luxury.

Short and thick?

Indicates brutality, gross instincts and low tastes. Can be a loyal minion, but makes a cruel tyrant.

Now, measure and compare the lengths of the first and the second phlanges of the thumb.

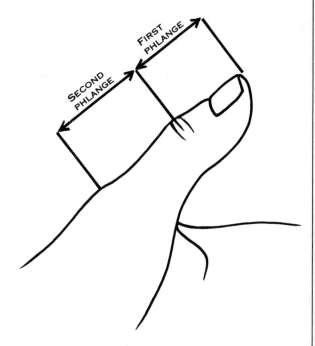

Is the 1st phlange

Shorter than the 2nd?

Logic rather than ambition or blind will-power guides the person with this characteristic. They make emotionally reasoned decisions which are usually very logical, and possess tact, charm and an ability to compromise.

Longer than the 2nd?

This signifies a predominance of will-power in the ego, one who is likely to be stubborn and unable to compromise. If very much longer, it can indicate a personality likely to conflict and disagree with others, an argumentative person who must have his or her own way, and cannot be reasoned with.

Are the two phlanges equal in length?

This is a sign of balance, where logic and will work together; a humane and sensitive person with a good combination of logic and will in decision-making.

Is the thumb 'waisted', i.e. narrow in the middle of the 2nd phlange when viewed front on?

As the 'waist' affects the phlange of logic, the subject may often act through emotional impulse. Traditionally, it also gives the subject an ability to deal with people diplomatically.

MARKS ON FINGERS

The markings on the fingers show specific talents and problems in certain areas. Because the phlanges relate to the 12 signs of the zodiac, these marks can be of particular use to astrologers.

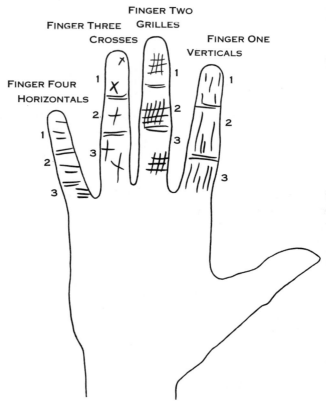

There are four commonly occurring marks:

Vertical lines — these are signs of positive energy. Astrologically, a good aspect.

Grilles — these are a mark of confused, undirected energy. Astrologically, grilles are possibly neutral.

Crosses — these signal misapplied, or diverted energy. Astrologically, a bad aspect.

Horizontal lines — these are stress marks and signal blocked energy. Astrologically, some form of retrograde activity is indicated.

Now, examine each finger, starting with the index, or Jupiter finger. Begin at the tip and read down toward the palm.

FINGER 1, PHLANGE 1: ARIES (I AM)

Does this phlange have

Verticals?

A sign of inspirational spiritual skills, religious fervour, leadership skills.

Grilles?

Incarceration, imprisonment or seclusion of some sort, possibly in a monastery, or in artistic isolation; one imprisoned by their beliefs.

Crosses?

Obsession, possibly religious or moral, which disturbs the subject's sense of reality.

Horizontals?

These are stress marks, indicating failure of religious aspirations, an inspiration block, distraction of vital energy into trivialities.

FINGER 1, PHLANGE 2: TAURUS (I HAVE)

Does this phlange have

Verticals?

Signifies noble and idealistic ambitions; one motivated by morals and ethical ideals.

Grilles?

Self-deception; lack of self-knowledge.

Crosses?

A disposition to envy; one with a tendency to lie, misinform, plot and manipulate others.

Horizontals?

Signs of stress indicating that high ideals and ethics are not being lived up to.

FINGER 1, PHLANGE 3: GEMINI (I THINK)

Does this phlange have

Verticals?

Strong executive drive, good organisational skills, plausibility.

Grilles?

Likelihood of abuse of personal power in personal and business life.

Crosses?

Exploitative manipulation of others.

Horizontals?

Stress due to frustration of, or lack of, ambition. No strong desire to obtain power despite pressure to achieve.

FINGER 2, PHLANGE 1: CAPRICORN (I THINK)

Does this phlange have

Verticals?

The subject feels a strong sense of responsibility (be it personal or civic), a strong sense of duty, and need of material security.

Grilles?

This signals a person conditioned to fail.

Crosses?

The mark of an instinctive, superstitious person, with the likelihood of antisocial tendencies (possibly taking the form of crimes to property).

Horizontals?

Stress due to the weight of responsibility, and perhaps a sense of failing in one's duty. This can also indicate being over-worked.

Finger 2, phlange 2: Aquarius (I know)

Does this phlange have

Verticals?

A sign of academic ability and scientific interests; one interested in 'truth'.

Grilles?

A defeatist with a pessimistic or fatalistic attitude that makes any progress difficult and unlikely.

Crosses?

A mark of one with a cold and detached attitude based on a distorted view of reality. He or she may also be eccentric or bigoted.

Horizontals?

Stress caused by academic pressures. This can also indicate a turning away from consensus reality; taking refuge in cultivated ignorance.

Finger 2, phlange 3: Pisces (I believe)

Does this phlange have

Verticals?

A person with good common sense and financial abilities, with a love of security and comfort; often actively seeking self-development.

Grilles?

>A confused person with little common sense, and incapable of judging his or her own abilities and limitations.

Crosses?

>A sign of self-development diverted towards sterile or trivial ends.

Horizontals?

>Stress caused by poor attitudes and behaviour; a friendless or unlucky person, lacking common sense.

FINGER 3, PHLANGE 1: CANCER (I FEEL)

Does this phlange have

Verticals?

>Signifies an extreme form of sensitivity, possibly artistic genius; one with a high order of creative skills, originality and energy.

Grilles?

>A sign that sensitivity has scrambled to a painful intensity, provoking retreat, withdrawal and depression.

Crosses?

>Creativity has been diverted into trivial or antisocial ends.

Horizontals?

>A sign of stress caused by some obstacle to the free and inspired expression of creative talent.

FINGER 3, PHLANGE 2:
LEO (I WILL)

Does this phlange have

Verticals?

> The sign of an outwardly expressive artist, competitive and with a keen appreciation of commercial aspects.

Grilles?

> The mark of an envious, frustrated artist who lacks insight and sensitivity.

Crosses?

> Talent diverted into trival ends.

Horizontals?

> Stress caused by obstacles to the flow of artistic expression.

FINGER 3, PHLANGE 3:
VIRGO (I ANALYSE)

Does this phlange have

Verticals?

> Analysis and perception; the mark of the artisan or craftsman, who pays attention to detail and has a drive to achieve perfection.

Grilles?

> A sign of perfection heightened to the point of obsession; a nagging, picky perfectionist.

Crosses?

> Need of perfection centred on the self, and doomed to failure; self-punishment.

Horizontals?

> Stress; obstacles hampering the free flow of creative energy.

FINGER 4, PHLANGE 1:
LIBRA (I BALANCE)

Does this phlange have

Verticals?

A skilled communicator; eloquent, diplomatic and tactful. This person has a love of harmony and luxury.

Grilles?

A mark of poor skills of communication.

Crosses?

A sign that communication skills are used for selfish motives.

Horizontals?

Stress caused by some hindrance to self-expression; a boaster.

FINGER 4, PHLANGE 2:
SCORPIO (I DESIRE)

Does this phlange have

Verticals?

These indicate a person with developed sexual communication skills; a deep, sincere and passionate person. A sign of potency and fertility.

Grilles?

A sign of poor sexual communication skills.

Crosses?

One whose sexual communication skills are used in a negative way; a person who is sexually aggressive, predatory, cunning and selfish.

Horizontals?

Stress caused by problems in sexual communication. They can also indicate infertility or gynaecological disorders.

FINGER 4, PHLANGE 3: SAGITTARIUS (I SEE)

Does this phlange have

Verticals?

> An articulate and truthful communicator, with good skills of salesmanship.

Grilles?

> The sign of tactless communicators; people who always seem to have their feet in their mouths.

Crosses?

> A compulsive exaggerator and liar.

Horizontals?

> Stress indicating inarticulate expression, leading to misunderstanding.

THE THUMB, PHLANGE 1

Does this phlange have

Verticals?

> A sign of a strong will, energy, confidence and strength; one whose will is often obeyed.

Grilles?

> A mark of scattered will-power — energy diverted into trivial and unimportant matters.

Crosses?

> A sign of unusual obstinacy, mindless stubbornness and inability to compromise.

Horizontals?

> These are stress marks, bars to the free expression of will, and show someone whose will is often thwarted, who lacks confidence.

THE THUMB, PHLANGE 2

Does this phlange have

Verticals?

A sign of good powers of logic and reasoning, and common sense.

Grilles?

Flawed powers of reasoning; dishonesty; one who rationalises their dishonesty.

Crosses?

Signifies twisted rationalising of one's actions, motives, etc.

Horizontals?

Stress indicating lack of common sense and barriers to the free application of logic and reason.

THE THUMB, PHLANGE 3

Does this phlange have

Verticals?

Vitality; intense emotional and physical feelings; a love of life, relationships and family. This also can signify assistance given to the subject by others in a close, supportive relationship.

Grilles?

A mark of one with a passionate disposition, yet with some confusion regarding sexual and emotional priorities.

Crosses?

A sign of emotional obsession. (The traditional reading is of 'an only love; a single, all-absorbing passion'.)

Horizontals?

A sign of stress, usually indicating interference or influence of another in sexual and family relationships.

THE LINES

The major lines

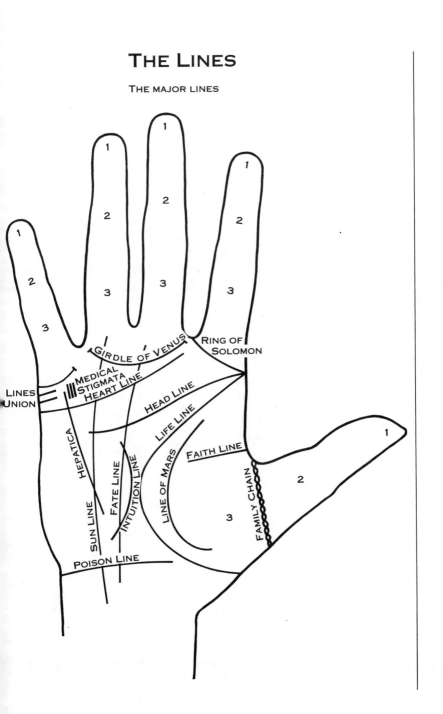

THE LIFE LINE

The Life Line, also called the *Vital*, re-spresents the physical self and shows general health, vitality and physical interaction with the environment.

Is the Line

Clear, well defined and long — reaching, or almost reaching the wrist?

> This signifies health, vitality and energy. It also shows the optimism and positive outlook of someone with good coping skills, who adapts well to changes. It promises a long and generally healthy life.

Broken in one or more places?

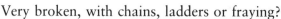

> Breaks signify disruptions to the physical self. They can also be an indication of acute illness, or sudden change in circumstances, such as the quitting of an old lifestyle and the begin-ning of a new. The change may be positive or negative depending on the condition of the line after the break.

Very broken, with chains, ladders or fraying?

> This is a sign of uncertain health, low vitality and energy levels, exhaustion and poor pow-ers of recuperation. It suggests a life of much disruption, change and difficulty.

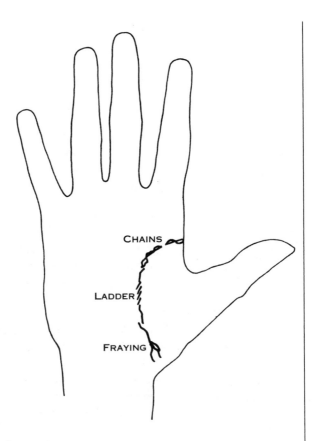

CHAINS

LADDER

FRAYING

Marked with islands?

Islands are traditionally negative and indicate periods of ill-health. They may also represent periods of 'split energy' which can occur when the subject is experiencing a period of discontentment, due to an unhappy marriage, unpleasant work, and so on.

Apparently double, with parallel lines?

This is a sign of strength, an enduring constitution, and strong recuperative powers. It may also indicate endemic dissatisfaction with routine, a need to continually seek changes in circumstances, restlessness, and a need of personal freedom. It can signify the extent of spiritual and emotional support given by a companion or spouse who provides love and assistance, and the degree to which the subject is dependent on that person.

It also tells of an intense sexual and emotional life. When the Life Line is clearly double, the subject has an 'inner' and an 'outer' life which are distinctly separate. This is occasionally found in people with jobs that require a professional persona.

Crossed by small lines?

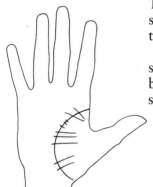

These are lines of influence, and usually represent other people. This influence may be negative or positive.

If there are many lines, they indicate the susceptibility of the subject to influence, betraying a submissive personality or a lack of self-confidence.

Short — only reaching the centre of the palm?

Often symptomatic of a personality lacking in colour, vitality, and significant events in his or her life.

This signifies a monotonous life, and may also mean the subject has ceased to make any effort to improve, and finds life 'too much'. Withdrawal and lack of involvement

is also indicated. Length is related to energy levels rather than time.

If the line is short and faded, non-involvement and withdrawal is indicated.

If the line is short and strong, intense self-absorption is indicated.

Long — reaching the wrist?

A sign of great physical vitality, with good powers of recuperation; probability of a long and healthy life; and an optimistic, healthy outlook.

Thick and red?

This shows a high level of physical vitality and energy. If very red, a violent and physical nature, irritable and excitable.

Pale and thin?

This marks low levels of physical vitality and energy; weakness due to stress generated by personal problems; and poor health due to lack of vitamins and/or essential body salts.

Slightly curved, clinging to the base of the thumb?

A sign of one who is family oriented and fond of domestic life. It may also indicate restriction, discontentment and a lack of warmth and vitality. This person may be timid and conservative; shy and uninterested in change and travel.

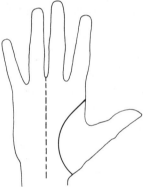

Steeply curved, reaching well into the palm?

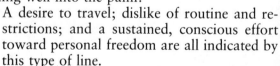

A desire to travel; dislike of routine and restrictions; and a sustained, conscious effort toward personal freedom are all indicated by this type of line.

It also shows a life strongly influenced by emotion and the subconscious, and indicates vitality, resilience and warmth of one who may be inclined towards a spiritual search for Truth.

Does the line

Change direction suddenly?

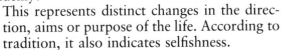

This represents distinct changes in the direction, aims or purpose of the life. According to tradition, it also indicates selfishness.

Begin touching the Head Line?

Touching for less than 1 cm: a mark of average mental and physical development, with strong family influence in childhood.

Touching for more than 1 cm: a sign of lack of independence, restrictions in early life due to parental domination, self-consciousness and lack of self-confidence.

This can also indicate health, educational or environmental problems — a subject cautious and reserved, with a fear of commitment.

The longer the join, the greater the above characteristics and influence.

Begin well separated from the Head Line?

This signals independence and a need for personal freedom. An impulsive person holding firm opinions; energetic and self-reliant, with managerial talents.

If very widely separated, there may be a lack of self-discipline, and the ideals of independence may be taken to extremes resulting in rash action, foolhardiness, impatience — grand ideas but very little action.

A fine network of lines between the Life and the Head lines usually indicates family resistance to the individuality and independence of the subject.

Begin above the Head Line?

A sign of a very cautious, timid nature, prone to worry and lacking self-confidence; someone who is too open to influence and domination by others and whose intellectual energy is under-employed. Often irritable, the subject is generally ruled by emotion rather than logic and reason.

Begin with an irregularity, branch or island?

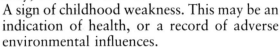

A sign of childhood weakness. This may be an indication of health, or a record of adverse environmental influences.

End well across the palm, towards the percussion?

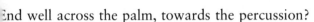

Wanderlust, restlessness and travel are all indicated.

The subject may be disinclined towards family life, disliking routine, and seeking change.

This can also indicate spiritual leanings.

End in a fork?

Signifies possible changes in old age; general restlessness; a love for, indeed need of, travel and change. It may also indicate 'late-blooming' — increased possibilities in late middle age.

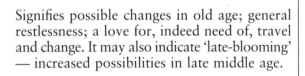

Branch upward, towards the fingers?

A symbol of replenished energy and happiness due to increases in influence and personal power. This may also indicate an effort to further personal ambitions or to improve oneself.

Branch down, towards the wrist?

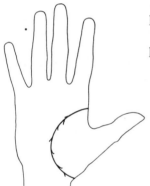

This shows a diminishing or splitting of vital physical energy.

It may signal a difficulty or a loss — personal or material.

THE HEAD LINE

This line, also called the *Mental*, represents the intellectual self and shows the degree and character of the intelligence, reasoning powers, the ability to concentrate and learn, and mental activity in general.

Is the line

Clear, well defined and long? (The line is 'long' if it reaches more than halfway across the palm.)

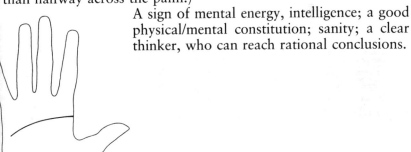

A sign of mental energy, intelligence; a good physical/mental constitution; sanity; a clear thinker, who can reach rational conclusions.

Broken in one or more places?

Breaks tend to impede thinking, and affect the ability to concentrate, and can indicate mental stress or breakdown. They can also represent a complete change in the way of thinking: a shift from an established viewpoint to a new set of mental values. Furthermore, breaks can indicate a physical injury to the head, or a severe shock.

Very broken, with chains, ladders or fraying?

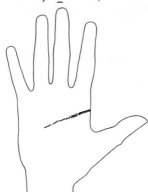

A sign of an inability to concentrate or reach rational conclusions. An indecisive and easily distracted subject who lacks continuity of ideas, and so appears to be changeable and fickle. The subject may be prone to mood swings.

This can also be an indication of acute trauma or severe mental stress.

Marked with islands?

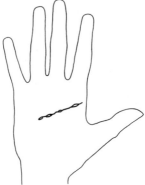

Islands represent a split in energy flow, and thus represent a period of difficulty and confusion, with much indecision and uncertainty. They can also represent trauma, whether it be actual psychosis or mental breakdown.

Very straight?

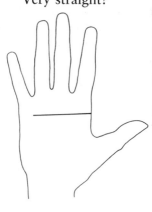

Signifies numeracy, a materialistic outlook, rational judgement; a person who is generally analytical in outlook and approach to life; and who is incisive and decisive, with application to detail.

This subject may have a tendency to ignore or discount emotional considerations when making decisions.

Curved, either up or down?

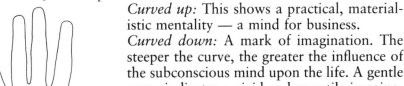

Curved up: This shows a practical, material-istic mentality — a mind for business.

Curved down: A mark of imagination. The steeper the curve, the greater the influence of the subconscious mind upon the life. A gentle curve indicates a vivid and versatile imagina-tion, with a tendency to daydream. When the curve is very steep, the subconscious influence is powerful. It can show a tendency to with-draw from everyday reality and can indicate (a) potential or actual psychosis, (b) artistic and creative ability, or (c) deep spirituality.

Changing direction suddenly?

Suggests an erratic, changeable mentality. The subject may use odd reasoning methods in decision-making, confusing the obvious and pertinent with the obscure and irrelevant. Possibly superstitious, the subject may place great emphasis on unimportant factors, mak-ing behaviour difficult to understand.

Very long — reaching more than halfway across the palm?

The line is long if it ends beneath fingers 3 or 4. This shows the subject to be intelligent, observative, understanding, and in possession of a positive outlook on life, with a keen sense of logic and good learning abilities.

Very short — does not reach more than halfway across the palm?

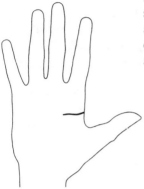

Indicates the lack of vision and imagination of someone who has fixed ideas, is obsessive, and has very narrow, strictly practical interests. It may also indicate a frivolous personality, lacking in depth and curiosity.

Joined to the Heart Line, so that it makes one line reaching across the entire palm?

Here the streams of intellectual and emotional energy have joined, giving great mental energy, emotional intensity and stamina. The result is an intense, headstrong and self-willed personality (the Traditional reading suggests a violent, uncontrollable character), who feels a need for total commitment in work, play and relationships.

There may at times be a confusion of energies, and of logic and emotions. The subject may tend to 'think' with feelings and feel through logic, leading to inappropriate behaviour — e.g. an emotional manager, a rational lover.

It is also an indication of Down's Syndrome.

So long that it crosses the entire palm?

This is symptomatic of a self divided into emotional and intellectual halves, leading to strictly logical reasoning with no emotional input, and/or emotional behaviour with no logical input.

Great insight is indicated, with an ability to reason without emotional interruption; however, problems may arise from this lack of integration between emotional and logical considerations, and this often results in the suppression of the emotional and imaginative aspects of the personality.

Traditionally, this is an indication of high intelligence which can lead to fame.

Steeply curved, so that it runs parallel to the Life Line?

The influence of the subconscious is very powerful in the subject with this feature, and this can lead to over-sensitivity or paranoia, along with some confusion between the imagined and reality. It very often indicates (a) artistic and creative powers; (b) psychosis, actual or potential; or (c) deep spirituality, with possible psychic or clairvoyant powers.

Red?

A sign of a dynamic and strong will. If very red, high energy verging on hyperactivity is indicated, and, possibly, a violent nature.

Very pale?

Indicates mental fatigue and lack of energy, and possibly a lack of essential body salts. The subject may be under psychological stress.

Does the line

Begin just touching the Life Line?

> Shows normal mental development in child-hood; a good start to life.

Begin separated from the Life Line and well into the palm?

> A lack of positive formative influences is suggested, along with a lack of family pride or involvement.
>
> Possibly a late developer, the subject may be uninterested in conventional achievement.

End in a fork?

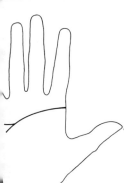

Denotes great imagination, via conscious access to subconscious processes, and an ability to make dreams come true. This is also a sign of artistic ability and creativity, and is traditionally called the poet's or writer's fork.

The subject is capable of viewing situations from two sides, which can mean duplicity.

If the fork is very steep and long, it may indicate an over-active imagination with its attendant problems, or a leaning towards spirituality, with some psychic ability.

End curved up at the tip?

Signals a desire for material gain of someone with a practical turn of mind and business acumen.

THE HEART LINE

This line, also called the *Mensal*, represents the emotional self and shows the degree and type of emotional experience, and the way it is expressed.

Is the line

Clear, well defined and long? (The Heart Line is 'long' if it reaches more than halfway across the palm.)

The subject is capable of strong, firm affections and self-sacrifice in relationships. He or she will be emotionally mature, emotionally self-confident.

There is a probability of a lifestyle that promotes stable relationships and has spiritual purpose.

Broken in one or more places?

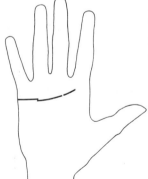

A sign of a break in the flow of emotional energy; a change in emotional attachments, which may indicate disappointment or disillusionment in love; can indicate, quite literally, a 'broken heart'.

Very broken, with chains, ladders or fraying?

The subject is emotionally immature or uncertain, lacks love for self, and is unconvinced of his or her own attractiveness.

This subject is attracted to novelty and change, needs constantly to renew excitement, and is likely to be fickle.

Marked with islands?

A sign of insecurity; of someone who is always actively seeking fulfilment. Brooding periods with depression are symptomatic of this characteristic, along with an active discontent with relationships.

Many islands can indicate a flirtatious character — a person who perhaps has many affairs. It can sometimes indicate a contempt for the opposite sex (arising out of contempt for self), and difficulty in trusting a sexual partner, again due to mistrust of self.

This may also indicate a heart condition.

Intersected by short, small lines?

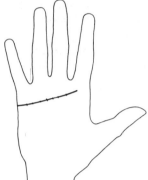

The number of these small influence lines is a measure of the influence of others upon the subject — or the subject's capacity to be influenced.

They can also represent a constantly shifting emotional focus (hence the traditional reading of promiscuity), inconstancy, and a series of flirtatious affairs.

Quite straight?

If *short*: a sign of calculating, undemonstrative emotional nature; selfish sensuality.

If *long* (reaching to base of finger 1): signifies a humanistic, idealistic and undemonstrative emotional nature; someone whose response tends to be intellectual rather than emotional, yet is usually erotic.

Curved (especially at the end)?

Signals a warm, impulsive and physically demonstrative nature; one with a strong need to express affection physically and sexually, and who may be jealous and possessive.

Changing direction suddenly?

This can indicate a change in the basic emotional nature, along with obscure emotional reasoning whereby trivialities become confused with more important considerations.

This can make the subject's emotional decisions and reactions difficult for others to understand. Tradition calls this a sign of a selfish and self-gratifying person.

Very pale?

A sign of low energy levels: the subject may be emotionally indifferent or self-sufficient, and possibly asexual.

It may also indicate a lack of essential vitamins, minerals or body-salts.

Red in colour?

This suggests high levels of emotional energy; an emotionally passionate, intense and possibly violent nature. There may also be an indication of a cardiac condition and/or high blood pressure.

Does the line

Begin at the percussion (i.e. the edge of the hand)?

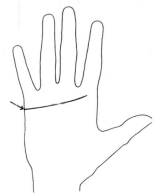

This is a sign of the normal emotional development of a sentimental person; one who is capable of giving and taking, and loving.

Begin anywhere other than the percussion?

Some interference with early emotional development is indicated; a disturbance of emotional character that has a lasting influence. It can mean the subject has developed a calculating, emotionally self-centred nature as a form of self-preservation.

End under finger 1?

This typifies the reliable, devoted type with a capacity for one consuming love. Faithful, and devoted to the highest ideals of humanistic love, this person may nevertheless be undemonstrative. Easily hurt, due to idealism on the battlefield of love, he or she is generally an affectionate, happy and promiscuous person.

End between fingers 1 and 2?

This represents the ideal, of one with a warm, generous, sympathetic and affectionate nature. Tending to physical displays of emotions, and an active role in relationships, this is a healthy balance between romantic idealism and sensuality.

This person is probably jealous and possessive, indicating an affinity for long-term relationships, such as marriage.

End under finger 2?

An unsentimental and undemonstrative person, for whom emotion figures in a minor key.

This personality is likely to have no strong feelings for others, and possess an element of unsentimental, self-centred sensuality in sexual relationships.

End under finger 3?

This person may feel little emotion and be extremely cautious when it comes to emotional involvement, possibly due to lack of strong emotional drive.

He or she may feel the need to maintain distance within a relationship and may be entirely motivated by sexual reasons.

End in a fork?

A sign that love and involvement are important to the subject, who is emotionally intense.

The person with this feature is likely to possess strong, honest feelings, and very often have a humanitarian outlook.

A triple fork (trident) is considered a very fortunate sign that the subject is capable of happy and passionate romantic attachments.

End joined to the Head Line?

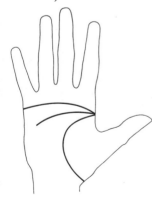

A sign of confused reason, emotion and instinct. This is often the mark of an emotionally dependent person in need of constant support, approval and affection from a partner.

He or she is most likely to be very sensitive to atmosphere and nuance.

...ie closer to the fingers than to the Head Line?

Shows a wide gap between emotional and intellectual energies. This can lead to a life-style dictated by logic and reason, with little emotional input or, conversely, one based on emotions, with little intellectual input.

THE FATE LINE

This line, also called the *Saturnian*, represents career and material achievement. It is also known as the career line, or the 'path of life' line. This line can be difficult to locate, as it often exists in fragmentary form and is easily confused with other lines. The best way to locate it is to trace it downwards from the base of finger 2. Many people do not have a fate line.

Is the line

Absent?

A sign that the subject has no discernible path in life, and is not forced or constrained to follow any particular path by family, or influences of education and environment. He or she is likely to have the attitude of taking life as it comes.

In a weak hand it indicates an aimless outlook, a character overly subject to outside influence.

Clear, long and well-defined?

Indicates a single, direct and straight path through life.

The subject probably has a strong sense of duty, coupled with a fatalistic, determined attitude. This is also called the career line as it can indicate the probability of success in a material sense and in the sphere of business. However, it can also simply mean the following of a single life-path, whether it leads to success or not.

Broken in one or more places?

Breaks represent changes in career or life-path. Many breaks show many changes, which can be negative or positive. How the line continues after each break indicates how the change has been adapted to.

Marked with islands?

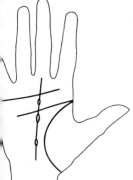

Islands are usually negative. They indicate split energies, and here signal a temporary weakening effect.

They are also a sign of stress, showing difficulties in career.

Intersected by small lines?

A sign of a sensitive character stressed by the demands of career or chosen path of life. This person may appear to be distant and detached.

Very curved or bent?

This signifies, literally, a curved and bent path through life; many changes of direction.

Double, or with parallel lines?

A mark of versatility or skills which may lead to a double career, and of more than one path or career being pursued at one time.

Does the line

Begin right at the base of the palm, so that it runs the length of the palm?

This is an indication of a strong genetic or cultural inheritance. The subject has been following his or her pre-determined path since birth.

Begin in the middle of the palm?

This represents the start of a career, or of some particular course (such as a spiritual direction), or the discovery and embracing of a lifestyle, which occurs in the early to mid-twenties.

Begin in contact with the Life Line?

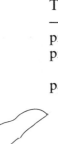

This shows an inheritance — genetic or family — that creates a lifepath; and expectation or pressure by family and relatives to follow a predetermined career.

It can also indicate domination by parents, family or spouse.

Begin with a fork?

A small fork at the very beginning shows that a choice was available at the beginning. A larger fork, with the joining point higher in the palm, shows the entrance into the life of a major influence.

It is often an indication of marriage.

Begin on Mount 8 (Mount of the Moon)?

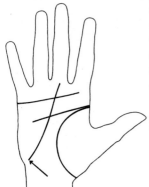

Denotes one who needs to express creativity, and who is hopeful and imaginative. The career of this person will depend on others to succeed (e.g. public life, show business, sport). May be unconventional and adventurous, with a love of travel and change.

The subject may also be largely unaware of his or her true motivation and ambitions, and can at times be deeply spiritual.

End under finger 1?

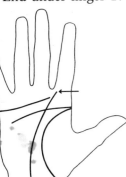

Shows driving ambition that is gratified at the end of a determined path, and a strong probability of material and career success.

End under finger 2?

Probability of career success; an ability to take advantage of opportunities. This is the usual termination point of the line.

End under finger 3?

Artistic ambitions and career are indicated — probably talent in the area of literature, art or music; inclination towards an artistic lifestyle.

End under the Heart Line?

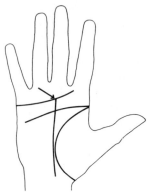

This signals a career or life-path interrupted or curtailed by emotional considerations, such as stress engendered by career success.

End at the Head Line?

Depending on other aspects of the hand, this can signify (a) a career or life-path interrupted or curtailed by intellectual considerations or stress engendered by success in career, and/or (b) someone whose life is strictly controlled by parents or spouse.

End in the middle of the palm?

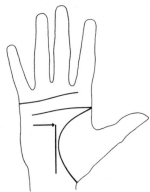

This may mean the subject has succeeded in breaking out of a narrow, restricting life-path, and achieved freedom of choice.

However, the traditional reading is of career failure after a good start; a failure to recognise or exploit opportunities.

THE SUN LINE

This line, also called the *Apollo* line, traditionally represents artistic success and recognition. It is also called the 'line of brilliance' and is related to probability of achievement and the attainment of contentment. Like the Fate line, it can be quite different to locate. Although it runs up the palm, the best way to locate it is to trace it downwards from the base of finger three. It generally exists in a fragmentary form. Many people do not have a Sun line.

Is the line

Absent?

Subjects without a Sun Line may have creative talents and artistic ability, but lack qualities such as ambition and business acumen to achieve recognition and success in the creative arts.

Clear, long and well-defined?

The subject is capable of success and recognition in a chosen field, particularly the creative arts, and is a basically happy, contented person.

A sign, also, of successful application of natural talent and brilliance — hence the traditional name, the 'Line of Brilliance'.

Broken in one or more places?

Denotes interruptions or breaks in the progress of artistic development and evolution, a scattering or dissipation of artistic energy, and hindrances to recognition and success.

Marked with islands?

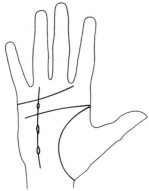

A sign of split energies, distraction and dissatisfaction, and of problems that interfere with career and artistic development.

The traditional reading is of loss of position, and scandal.

6

Does the line

Begin at the Heart Line?

Signifies the capable application of knowledge (often esoteric) gained in early life, leading to a measure of fame and success in middle age. This is the mark of a lateral thinker who makes major decisions based on emotional considerations. A late starter, whose influence has taken time to grow, the subject probably lacks driving ambition, has a love of art and beauty, and probably little interest in material gain.

Begin at the Head Line?

A sign of probable success and recognition, beginning in early middle age (around 40 years). Some traditions call this a sign of genius, suggesting that success arises from some intellectual inspiration or effort.

Begin at the Life Line?

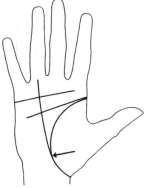

This represents probable success that is fostered with assistance from parents or family, or by some inheritance, genetic or otherwise.

Begin at the Fate Line?

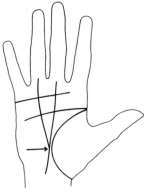

This signals a new life-path that arises from the career or the normal life-path of the subject. It could be a hobby that gradually 'takes over', or some other passionate interest that takes more and more time and energy. This can also represent an emergence, after repression, of artistic talents and ambitions.

Begin in the centre of the palm?

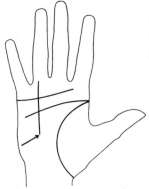

A sign that the life-path or artistic career of the subject does not start until his or her mid-twenties. Difficulties in choosing a path that satisfies creative leanings are also indicated.

End at the base of finger 3?

> The subject possesses qualities and talents that make artistic recognition and creative success a strong probability.

End at the Heart Line?

> This represents a creative path abandoned due to emotional stress which may be the result of either success or failure and frustration in the working life.
>
> It can also indicate a tendency to base crucial decisions on emotional considerations, often to the detriment of the practical.

End at the Head Line?

> Represents a creative path abandoned due to mental and intellectual stress resulting from success or failure and frustration in the working life.

End in a fork?

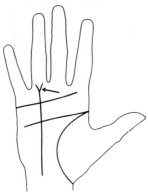

A sign of additional subjects or interests taken up in middle age and maturity. Traditional readings suggest outstanding success and recognition, probable wealth.

End in the middle of the palm, below the Head Line?

A creative pathway fades out. Tradition has it that this is a sign of early success, followed by stagnation.

THE UNION LINE

This line, also called the *marriage* line, represents the occurrence and extent of emotional commitment. These lines usually represent a commitment to another person, but may also signal commitment to a career or a cause.

Is the line

Absent?

A mark of emotional immaturity. The subject is currently not capable of making a major emotional commitment to a person or cause.

Straight and clear?

This is the ideal line, representing happy, intense and generally satisfying emotional involvement and commitment. Traditionally this means a happy marriage.

More than one line does not necessarily imply more than one marriage, as the union line can also represent commitment to a career or a cause.

Cut by fine lines?

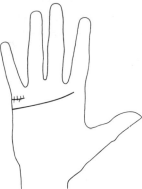

A sign of obstacles and opposition in emotional relationships. These lines can also represent fertility, and/or the desire to have children. Tradition has it that lines that go up towards the fingers indicate boys, and lines that go down show girls.

Marked by islands?

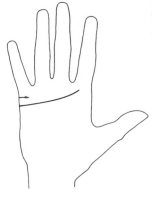

Islands indicate problems and difficulties in the relationship; possibly enforced separation, or split loyalties.

Does the line

End in a fork?

This signifies an extreme, intense form of emotional commitment, possibly a marriage with many quarrels or disagreements, or a love/hate relationship.

It can also imply a broken commitment, or an unhappy relationship which ends in separation.

This is also a sign of waning sexual interest in marriage, disillusionment with a commitment.

End with a downward curve, towards the Heart Line?

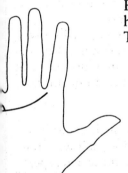

Represents enforced separation; a person who has difficulties maintaining their commitment. Traditionally this has signified widowhood.

End with an upward curve, towards the fingers?

The subject is unlikely to stick with major emotional commitments. The difficulty in maintaining relationships arises out of conditioning, education or experience.

Have a fine line, parallel and close by?

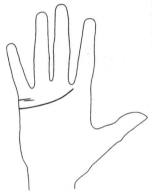

A sign of an emotional commitment made shortly after marriage. It may indicate a person, a cause or a career. It very often indicates commitment to children.

THE HEPATIC LINE

This line, also called the *Health* Line, the *Liver* Line and the *Hepatica*, can represent a health condition or a preoccupation with health. This line may be difficult to locate and is best traced downwards from beneath the 4th finger. Unlike the Sun and Fate lines, it runs diagonally across the palm.

Some traditions call this the Line of Mercury, and regard it as the 'business' line, to be read as an indication of a person's business life, following the normal rules that apply to reading lines.

Is the line

Absent?

The absence of the Hepatica, or Health Line, is considered a positive indication regarding health and constitution.

Furthermore, business is not a major concern in the subject's life.

Long, straight and well defined?

Here is a warning of some chronic health problem. (Traditional meaning: liver and digestive problems.) It can also signal one who is overly conscious of their health, and is possibly a hypochondriac.

In addition, it may be a sign of healing ability, most notably when the line forms a clear triangle in the centre of the palm with the Head and Fate or Life lines.

In addition, this person has a probable talent for business, and a strong possibility for success in business.

Very curved and/or bent?

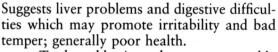

Suggests liver problems and digestive difficulties which may promote irritability and bad temper; generally poor health.

Trade and business do not run smoothly for this person.

Pale and wide?

Chronic digestion problems; poor circulation. A slow-moving career is indicated; hard work with minimal profits.

Red?

Cardiac problems. A difficult business life.

Crossed by small lines?

Migraine headaches. A business life beset by many problems and difficulties.

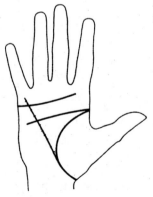

Does the line

Have islands?

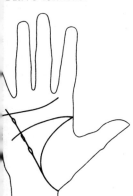

Chronic respiratory problems. Major set-backs in business; prolonged periods of recession.

Begin at the Heart Line?

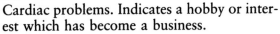

Cardiac problems. Indicates a hobby or interest which has become a business.

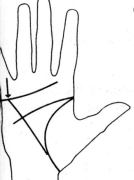

Begin at the Head Line?

A sign of nervous tension and susceptibility to stress.

The Mounts

The mounts are raised areas on the palm which represent different areas of the psyche, e.g. the libido, the subconscious, and so forth. Development (or the lack of) in the mounts sounds a base note by which all the other characteristics of the hand are modified. Sometimes, one or two mounts will be larger or more prominent than the rest, and clearly indicates the major motivating energy in the subject.

Take the subject's hand and examine each mount by touch as well as sight.

Position of the Mounts

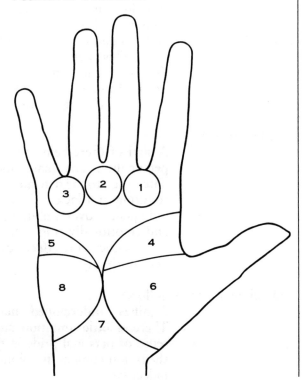

MOUNT 1:
JUPITER/SATURN (WIND)

Is the mount

Well developed, firm and high?

A sign of positive masculine qualities, corresponding to the Yang principle and the animus, and signifying personal power, pride, ambition and competitiveness.

This person has strong will-power, executive skills and personal ambition that can lead to a high position. In addition, he or she has a love of art, ritual and information.

Overdeveloped?

A sign of there being too much Yang in the personality. The masculine qualities dominate, often to the detriment of the Yin aspects, resulting in a lack of balance; a greedy, self-indulgent, over-ambitious, unsympathetic, and emotionally cold nature.

Other side-effects can include cynism and morbidity.

Undeveloped, flat or hollow?

Signifies undeveloped masculine qualities. There is little ambition and, if extreme, no sense of personal pride in this person. He or she is non-competitive, non-authoritarian and indecisive.

Crossed by vertical lines?

A sign of one attempting to improve his or her material position, in whom positive energy manifests as ambition, or a striving towards some goal.

If the Fate Line ends in this area, a strong probability of success is indicated.

Crossed by horizontal lines?

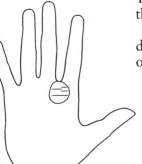

These are stress lines and show difficulties in the spheres of ambition and/or work.

Should the Heart Line end in this area, devotion and dedication to the higher ideals of love are indicated.

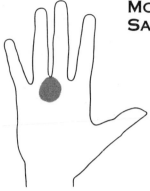

MOUNT 2:
SATURN/APOLLO (BEAUTY)

Is the mount

Well developed, firm and high?

> A sign that the subject has good powers of logical thought, proceeds steadily toward goals, an ability to complete things begun.
>
> It can also show a desire for knowledge, religious tendencies, and prudence. The subject is likely to have leadership qualities, a power to inspire trust in others, and patience and resignation.
>
> A mount of this kind can be a measure of financial success — some traditions call it the 'money bump'.

Overdeveloped?

> The qualities of intelligence and leadership can turn to arrogance, tyranny, bigotry and selfishness in someone with overdevelopment in this mount, resulting in a domineering nature, possibly devoted to material gain.

Undeveloped, flat or hollow?

> There is the likelihood of a defeatist, pessimistic attitude in this person, giving rise to failure which in turn feeds on itself, thereby creating a vicious circle.

He or she may have an inability to come to grips with or carry through a given task, and a general lack of commitment and effort.

Crossed by vertical lines?

An indication of positive energy and effort which can in turn promote favourable circumstances.

If the Fate Line ends in this area, vital energy that will last long into old age is suggested.

Crossed by horizontal lines?

These are stress marks and are a symptom of frustration or other problems in business or artistic life.

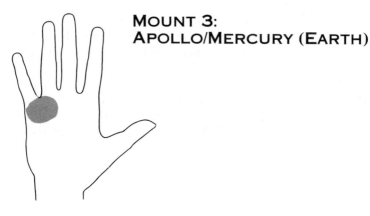

MOUNT 3:
APOLLO/MERCURY (EARTH)

Is the mount

Well developed, firm and high?

> This is a sign of positive feminine qualities corresponding to the Yin principle, and the anima.
>
> This person will be compliant, flexible and creative, with a cheerfully optimistic and generally accepting attitude.
>
> A good balance between artistic and practical talents is also indicated.

Overdeveloped?

> Signals exaggerated and distorted feminine qualities; negative communication qualities — artful dishonesty or outright lying.
>
> This person may be calculating, selfish, self-serving and pretentious.

Undeveloped, flat or hollow?

> A sign of an obstinate and impatient person with poor communication skills.
>
> He or she is probably impractical, without artistic or business skills, unsympathetic, and has poor sense of taste.

Crossed by vertical lines?

These are positive energy lines, representing artistic striving and the ability to overcome difficulties.

If the Sun Line ends here, it is a sign that artistic activity continues well into old age.

The Medical Stigmata may be present on this mount.

Crossed by horizontal lines?

These are stress marks indicating difficulties in the fields of work, communication or the arts.

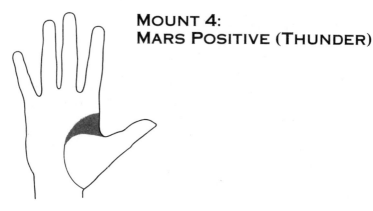

MOUNT 4:
MARS POSITIVE (THUNDER)

Is the mount

Well developed, firm and high?

> This mount represents the libido, the erotic and aggressive drive; the power of arousal, and emotional vitality.
>
> The strength or weakness of this mount affects all other aspects of the hand. It represents courage, self-control and the ability to cope with emergencies.
>
> A high degree of sexuality and strong sexual needs are also indicated.

Overdeveloped?

> A sign of aggression and high levels of sexual energy.
>
> If extreme, this can be an indication of cruelty, anger and tyranny; a bully, aggressive in all areas of life.

Undeveloped, flat or hollow?

> Signifies very low energy levels, a subdued and non-aggressive libido; possibly a timid, withdrawn character, lacking courage.

rossed by vertical or diagonal lines?

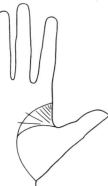

These are influence lines, representing the influence in early life of the subject's immediate family, and may be positive or negative. If negative, a confusion of lines, with islands, crosses, etc. will appear on the Life Line at the point of contact.

rossed by horizontal lines?

These are stress lines, indicating problems in the area of childhood development, that affect the entire hand, and the subject's life.

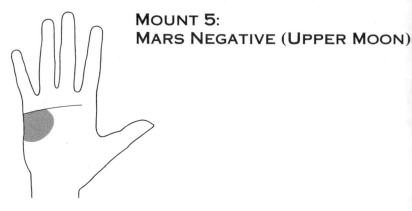

MOUNT 5:
MARS NEGATIVE (UPPER MOON)

Is the mount

Well developed, firm and high?

> This is a measure of the strength of a person's animal spirits, and capacity to enjoy day to day life.
>
> It shows that the subject takes pleasure in sex and procreation and has a love of relationships and domestic life. He or she enjoys food and drink, and physical activity.

Overdeveloped?

> The personality is governed by the animal spirits, which leads to sensuality with gross instincts and appetites — self-indulgence in food, sex and physical pleasures.

Undeveloped, flat or hollow?

> A sign of subdued animal spirits; of one with little energy for pleasure, domestic life or physical activity.
>
> This person may be dedicated to intellectual ideals and pleasures, and is possibly cool and unresponsive.

Crossed by vertical lines?

Verticals are always associated with positive energy. This is a person who devotes much effort to family, and whose life is rich and full of enjoyment. He or she probably regards having a good time as one of the more important considerations in life.

Crossed by horizontal lines?

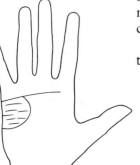

Signifies restlessness; stress in the area of life most affected by the animal spirits: family, courtship, pleasure and physical activity.

Tradition has it that this indicates travel.

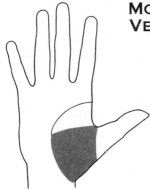

MOUNT 6:
VENUS (MOUNTAIN)

Is the mount

Well developed, firm and high?

> Ruled by Venus, this mount represents the conscious emotional quarter of the personality, and is the largest mount. It denotes a cheerful, optimistic personality, warm, generous, sympathetic, sociable and hospitable, with the capacity to enjoy life day to day.
>
> This person is affectionate and attractive, sexual and physical, and emotionally stable.

Overdeveloped?

> An indicator of excess sensuality, inconstancy, vanity and hedonism.
>
> This person takes great pleasure in physical relationships, has extreme emotional reactions, and a tendency towards violence.

Undeveloped, flat or hollow?

> A sign of suppressed emotions leading to coolness and inhibition in the expression of love and affection. Often egocentric, and apparently insensitive to the feelings of others, this person has little appreciation of beau-

ty or art, is pragmatic, with a view to the expedient, and quite frugal.

He or she has little enthusiasm for most things in life, and very little initiative.

Crossed by vertical lines?

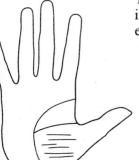

A sign of vitality and emotional energy, intense emotional and physical feelings, and the possibility of oversensitivity. This person has a love of life, relationships and family. Each line can also represent the assistance given by another in a close, supporting relationship, such as a spouse.

People with many verticals usually have a lust for freedom, and may have an interest in self-development.

Crossed by horizontal lines?

These are stress marks which may indicate interference or influence by other people, especially in sexual and family relationships.

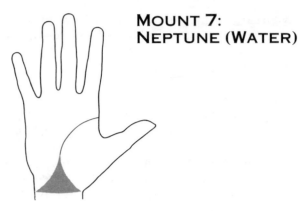

MOUNT 7:
NEPTUNE (WATER)

Is the mount

Well developed, firm and high?

> This mount forms a bridge between the conscious mind and the instinctive, bio-automatic, subconscious self. It shows that good interaction between left and right brains exists. People with this characteristic are compassionate, have a strong sense of self, the ability to communicate well on most levels, and an instinct for making correct decisions in most situations.

Overdeveloped?

> The sign of an overactive imagination; one who has a poor or distorted sense of reality, and may have difficulty in distinguishing between reality and fantasy.
>
> This person may also be self-centred and domineering.

Undeveloped, flat or hollow?

> This is a mark of people who are not in touch with their deeper motivations. They are largely unaware of their subconscious desires and motives, which can lead to a sense of personal conflict and feelings of angst and

dissatisfaction. Such people feel they should be doing something — only they don't know what.

Crossed by vertical lines?

A sign of positive energy. The Fate Line may begin on this mount, indicating there is a fixed path of life that will be followed from an early age.

Should the Life Line end here, a life of active mental and spiritual seeking is indicated, along with a strong likelihood of restlessness and wanderlust.

Crossed by horizontal lines?

These are stress marks and show a proneness to addiction and dependency.

They also suggest strong sensual desires, and a tendency to over-indulge.

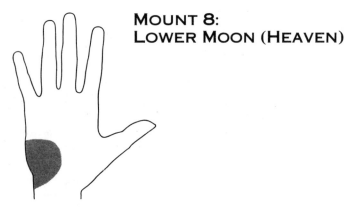

MOUNT 8:
LOWER MOON (HEAVEN)

Is the mount

Well developed, firm and high?

> Denotes the existence of an active subconscious mind, and a high degree of spiritual development.
>
> This person has a good sense of imagination, is refined, and has a talent for, or love of, poetry and music. He or she is attracted to change and travel.

Overdeveloped?

> This is a sign of a very active subconscious mind and a high level of creativity. When badly aspected, it hints at morbidity, paranoia, and a hyperactive imagination. It can also indicate psychosis.

Undeveloped, flat or hollow?

> Signifies an inactive subconscious and little imagination, and indifference to others. It denotes the inability to improvise and poor coping skills of one who is conservative, authoritarian, and dislikes change.

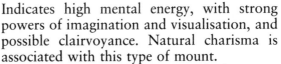

rossed by vertical lines?

Indicates high mental energy, with strong powers of imagination and visualisation, and possible clairvoyance. Natural charisma is associated with this type of mount.

The Line of Intuition usually begins in this area.

rossed by horizontal lines?

Signifies a loss of self-control and of a sense of reality.

If there is one straight, long line, the subject may be prone to addiction and dependence, with strong sensual desires, and a tendency to over-indulge.

Some traditions say that these horizontals are indications of travel, particularly of journeys overseas.

FURTHER DETAILS

These further details are subtleties that enhance and deepen the exploration of the character of the subject.

Examine the fingers of the subject when
he or she is in a relaxed attitude.

FINGERS

Is there a space between

Fingers 1 and 2?

A mark of courage and an ability to face
challenges. A generally dominant character
with good executive skills, who is self-
sufficient, independent and intolerant of the
foibles of others.

Fingers 2 and 3?

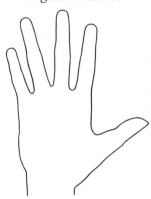

A sign of ambition and desire to be seen as
dominant or charismatic.

People with this characteristic often
have difficulty working with others, and will
probably have few friends. They lack fore-
thought, tend to live day to day, and have a
deep distrust of the motives of others, due to
mistrust of themselves.

Fingers 3 and 4?

An indication of a poor team-worker, in need of independence and privacy, who won't 'run with the herd'.

This person prefers his or her own company to that of others, and may be uncommitted in relationships.

Sexual and emotional immaturity, or social isolation are possible indications. The traditional reading suggests this as a sign of sexual perversion.

All the fingers?

An extrovert; gregarious, confident, and probably self-sufficient. This person has good powers of self-expression, and is possibly intolerant of the views of others.

The traditional reading is of a head-strong personality.

Look at the relative lengths of the fingers and their straightness.

Is finger 1 longer than finger 3?

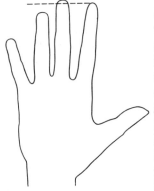

Longer: A naturally dominant personality, with possible leadership skills and executive ability; one who likes to have their own way in most situations. Often considered 'bossy', this personality has difficulty obeying orders or directions.

Shorter: A non-dominant character; not weak but rather, one who does not have a pathological need to be in control or command. Reasonably compliant and cooperative, this type is usually happy to let others take the lead.

Does finger 1 and/or 2 curve or bend toward finger 3?

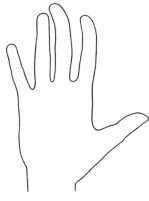

A sign that the conscious intellectual energies 'lean' towards the subconscious self. This person will generally allow his or her subconscious to make moral and practical decisions, i.e. the subject relies heavily on instinct, impulse and hunches in decision-making.

The traditional meaning is of an 'instinctive knowledge of right and wrong'.

Does finger 3 and/or 4 curve or bend toward finger 2?

An indication that the subject's subconscious creative energies are striving for expression; that he or she has an active subconscious.

This person may be either a visionary or a dreamer, and may have an awareness of the 'invisible world' of undefinable phenomena.

Now, observe the fingers held in a relaxed attitude to notice if any of them cling together.

Do fingers 1 and 2 cling together?

Denotes powers of leadership; however, the capacity to initiate action is hampered by an acute lack of self-confidence.

Do fingers 2 and 3 cling together?

An indication of self-abnegation and/or self-sacrifice, possibly due to the failure or frustration of dreams and ideals.

It can also mean repression: an artist forced to abandon the creative life, or a disillusioned romantic. Material and personal security may be a paramount consideration to the person with this characteristic.

Do fingers 1, 2 and 3 cling together?

A sign of dependence upon others. This feature characterises those in need of constant reassurance. They are sensitive to environmental influences and the surrounding atmosphere generally, and work well as team members.

They may have difficulties in expressing deeply personal ideas and feelings.

Do fingers 3 and 4 cling together?

Shows ambition and desire for leadership and personal power without the necessary ability for achievement.

This person wishes to lead and inspire, but is without the substance or inner resources to do so at the present time.

Do fingers 2, 3 and 4 cling together?

An ambitious person who is nevertheless lacking in aggressive drive; one who is likely to expend energy in areas where the competitive sense and aggression are not necessary for success.

Examine the pattern of the fingerprints on the tip of each finger and the thumb. Use a magnifying glass if you wish. There are four main patterns.

WHORL

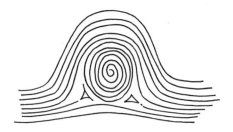

ARCH

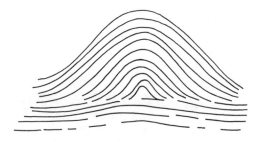

LOOP

TENTED ARCH

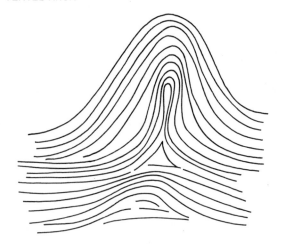

Any pattern that does not fall into these forms, or is a combination of two or more of these forms is a *composite*.

Is the pattern on finger 1

A whorl?

> A sign of individuality; a creative, active, unique character with leadership qualities and a dislike of publicity.

102

People with this pattern cling to their own views dogmatically and must be asked, not ordered.

A loop?

A charming, adaptable and thoughtful leader, who can nevertheless be most practical.

An arch?

Signifies a person entrenched in his or her own personal viewpoint; possibly of fanatic views. However, this person can be 'realistic' when it is for his or her own benefit.

A tented arch?

A sign of joie de vivre; an enthusiastic, youthful outlook.

A composite?

The mark of one lacking versatility and adaptability.

Is the pattern on finger 2

A whorl?

Indicates a hatred of routine; one who is analytical, sceptical, self-exploring and determined. This person may be hard to sway from his or her own viewpoint, self-sufficient, and self-protective.

A loop?

Practical, yet philosophical; one who is open-minded, honest, with a dislike of bias in others.

An arch?

Enjoyment and enthusiasm for work. Lack of an inner life, and inhibited. May avoid discussion of ideals.

A tented arch?

Idealistic, impractical. Caught up in speculation and philosophy.

A composite?

Basic and practical type, who is mentally uninspired and apathetic.

Is the pattern on finger 3

A whorl?

A sign of creativity, artistic ability, unconventional attitudes; this is nevertheless a self-controlled person whose feelings are based on well-defined and set patterns.

A loop?

Craftsmanship. Emotional and artistic freedom. Emotionally oriented, fashionable type.

An arch?

Love of science, precision and machinery; emotionally inarticulate. Can be obsessive.

A tented arch?

Emotional, highly-strung, artistic; one who has musical talent, personal flair and is enthusiastic but impractical.

A composite?

Utilitarian and philistine attitudes.

Is the pattern on finger 4

A whorl?

The sign of a rugged individualist who carefully selects everything in life with an eye to interest and pleasure. Hedonistic, charming and persuasive, this person is hard to influence.

A loop?

One who easily assimilates new ideas. Tactful and with good verbal skills, this person is a talker rather than a doer.

An arch?

A primitive survivalist, with a low level of communication skills.

A tented arch?

Indicates a flair for learning languages.

A composite?

A sign of poor language and communication skills.

Is the pattern on the thumb

A whorl?

The individualistic and original character, with a strong will and a very persevering nature.

A loop?

A practical, direct, deft, flexible person, with a diplomatic nature. May have a love of risk-taking.

An arch?

One who exhibits signs of indecision, suspicion and caution; yet has practical coping skills.

A tented arch?

A person with a flexible nature, who works and cooperates well with others, is charming, and has a tractable will.

A composite?

A sign of uncertainty; a slow moving and thinking person, but generally quite enduring and persevering.

Now, examine the palm for the minor lines shown in the following illustration.

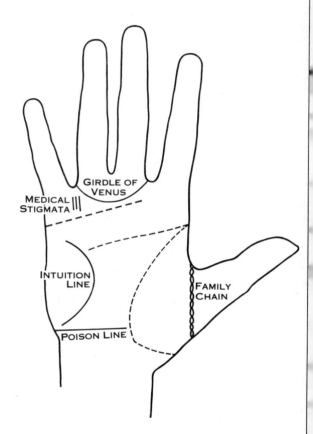

THE GIRDLE OF VENUS

Is the Girdle of Venus

Clear and well-defined?

> A sign of emotional hypersensitivity and sensuality — belonging to restless personalities in need of continuous (and sometimes artificial) emotional stimulation. He or she may be prone to extreme mood swings and possesses a naturally dependent nature, with a danger of addiction and dependency.

Also called the Line of Libido, it is traditionally considered to indicate prostitution, drug addiction and sexual perversion or promiscuity.

Broken in one or more places?

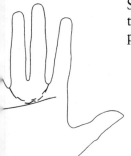

Signifies emotional hypersensitivity, a disturbed libido, and difficulties in achieving peace of mind and emotional fulfilment.

Very fragmented; only partially present?

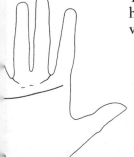

This shows a certain degree of emotional hypersensitivity — a person easily moved, and very emotional in outlook and action.

THE MEDICAL STIGMATA

Are the Medical Stigmata present?

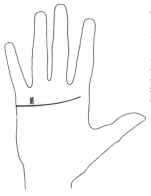

The sign of a healer, this indicates an aptitude for medical or healing professions.

They are also called the 'samaritan lines', and may indicate an ability to alleviate pain and discomfort by massage, laying on of hands, etc. or one with a healing personality.

THE INTUITION LINE

Is the Intuition Line present?

In a Water or Fire hand, this is a sign of psychic ability and clairvoyance.

In Earth and Air hands, this is a positive indication of an active and guiding intuition and instinct; a natural sixth sense.

THE FAMILY CHAIN

Is the Family Chain present?

This is said to indicate close family ties, and probably relates to dependence on family support and comfort.

This is the mark of one who functions best in the outside world from within the framework of a warm, tight family circle.

THE POISON LINE

Is the Poison Line present?

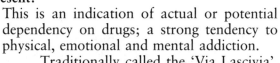

This is an indication of actual or potential dependency on drugs; a strong tendency to physical, emotional and mental addiction.

Traditionally called the 'Via Lascivia', it was supposed to indicate lax morals, sexual perversion and over-indulgence.

It can also indicate presence of some type of allergy.

NAILS

The condition and shape of the nails show personality characteristics and general health. Many common problems with nails, such as softness, splitting, white spots and so forth, derive from some form of malnutrition.

Are the nails

Bitten?

Bitten nails are generally more than just a bad habit: they are a sign of stress, which can indicate poor emotional balance, general irritability, intolerance, introspection and loneliness.

Bitten nails show that the subject is not coping or adjusting well to aspects of his or her life.

Wider than they are long (short nails)?

This is the sign of people with a very critical, logical and analytical approach to things. Often belligerent, argumentative and stubborn, they may have an unforgiving streak in their character, be self-righteous and narrow-minded.

If the nail is very wide, the subject may also be bad-tempered, aggressive and intolerant. It can also indicate a tendency to heart troubles.

Longer than they are wide (long nails)?

The sign of an easy-going person, intuitive, artistic and idealistic, who may lack physical energy, and tend to ignore unpleasant facts or events. They can be ironic and sarcastic, but are generally peace-loving and slow to anger.

This may also show a tendency to chest and lung complaints.

Wedge-shaped (narrow at the base, widening at the top)?

A sign of anxiety, and mental and nervous disorders; a person with poor 'nerves', and a disposition to worry. A tendency to nervous or mental exhaustion is also indicated.

Oval-shaped?

A sign of a courteous, refined, sweet and obliging nature — devoted and loyal. Honest, placid and generally peaceful, people with this feature are nevertheless prone to overly emotional outbursts when stressed.

Very long and narrow (like talons)?

The mark of people with selfish natures and little regard for others. Grasping and greedy, they are often very persistent in the pursuit of their aims. It can also indicate malnutrition.

Do the nails

Have moons?

With moons: A sign of a good physical constitution, and a contented mind. If the moon has a bluish halo, it can be a sign of vascular problems, and may be an early warning of a stroke.

Without moons: According to tradition, this indicates a poor physical constitution. Research is needed here.

Have vertical ridges?

'Senile nails' are very common in the elderly. They can be an indication of inherited rheumatism or arthritis, and are related to chronic stress and to Darier's Disease (a genetic skin disorder).

People undergoing radiation treatment often develop these ridges.

Have white spots?

> An indication of calcium deficiency. It may also indicate fatigue, tension, or malfunction of the liver. Tradition tells us that white spots are symptomatic of unfortunate love affairs.

Now, note the colour. Is the nail

Red?

> Hypertension; high blood pressure.

Pink?

> Normal; indicates good health.

Blue?

> Circulatory problems. If blue appears in the nails of one hand only, it can be an early warning of a stroke.

Very pale and colourless?

> Poor diet; malnutrition; acute symptom of shock. It may also indicate cirrhosis of the liver or kidney problems.

THE NOTES

The **Notes** contain essential information that supplements and enhances the **Workshop**. The ancient art and science of palmistry — the original and still the most accurate form of psychoanalysis — is not a quick study. There is a formidable mass of detail to be absorbed; however, a careful reading of the Notes, combined with use of the Workshop, will remove most of the difficulties usually associated with the study of palmistry.

Interpretation and Intuition

Having worked your way through the Workshop, you may finish with only a few *yes* answers, or a great many. Since each definition contains a statement about a characteristic, representing a single facet of a personality, the number of *yes* answers reflects how complex and multi-faceted the subject is.

Some of the answers will be contradictory, while others will complement and tend to confirm traits. Contradictory answers reflect conflict and contradiction in the subject. Most of us are a collection of traits, habits and characteristics mixed with conditioning that somehow all balance out to form our individual personalities.

It is important that you, as the palmist, take a holistic view of the subject's personality. *Yes* answers should never be considered in isolation, nor should too much weight be given to a single aspect. This is the golden rule of palmistry: marks and signs must be seen as a part of a functioning whole. Negative indications are often modified by more positive signs elsewhere on the hand.

The objective is to look at the subject as a whole, to view the mass of information, and to weigh it all up and see how it combines to make the subject the person he or she is.

Referral to the palmistic map of a person is a simple and non-threatening procedure, full of interest for the subject of the read and the reader. Just watch the reaction of your friends when you admit you are studying palmistry. Even the skeptics want a turn!

The hand displays a wealth of information. The art is to weave this information into a clear portrait — this is where intuition comes in.

INTUITION

Intuition constitutes the non-exact segment of the science and art of palmistry. Some of you will be gifted with intuition; others will, with practice, develop it. The information that feeds intuition comes from many sources: directly from the palm, for while you hold a subject's hand many subtle, unconscious impressions will be received; the age, sex, clothing and body language of the subject will also convey clues. Your own life-experience and knowledge will also contribute to your intuition about a particular subject.

It is important for the serious student to read as many palms as they possibly can. Intuition is a muscle that strengthens with regular exercise.

Eventually, accuracy and confidence will grow, as will knowledge, and the need to refer to the text will decrease.

Don't be afraid of making mistakes. Have confidence in the basic accuracy of palmistry. If a subject denies some aspect of themselves that is clearly marked on their hand, it is more often than not a measure of that subject's lack of self-knowledge.

Methodology

Left and Right Hands

There are a variety of opinions concerning which hand should be read: 'The future is shown in the right, the past in the left' is one such. 'Length of days is in her right hand, riches and honour are in her left' is a quote from the Bible (Proverbs 3:16). However, it is more usual to read the *right* hand. Custom has it that potential shows in the *left* hand, while the right hand shows the realised personality.

The saying goes that 'the left hand is the one we are born with, and the right is what we have made of it'.

Another has it that the right hand is read for men, while the left is read for women.

Helped by relatively recent developments in psychology, modern palmistry has been able to clarify and enhance more traditional readings.

The Significance of the Left Hand

The left hand is controlled by the right brain, which regulates pattern recognition, and understands the relationship between one thing and another. The left hand reflects the 'inner' person. It is the *yin* aspect of the personality, the feminine, receptive side of the self. It is the 'natural self', with an aptitude for art. It is the Anima, highly personal, intuitive and erotic. And it is lateral thinking.

The left may be considered as a record of an individual's personal and spiritual development.

THE SIGNIFICANCE OF THE RIGHT HAND

The right hand is controlled by the left brain, which regulates logic, reason and language, and understands detail and how things work. The right hand reflects the 'outer' person. It is the *yang* aspect of the personality, the masculine, active side of the self. It is the objective self and shows the influence of social environment, education and experience. It is concerned with practical, 'outward' matters, adaptation to society, the need to make a living. And it is lineal thinking.

The right hand may be seen as the individual's adaptation to the environment, and the influence of family and society.

COMPARE

It is always worthwhile to study a subject's hands together, taking care to note down any major differences between the left and right. The ideal would be to have left and right hands identical. The subject in such a case would prove a very balanced and integrated person, with an inner self matched to the outer personality. This is fairly rare, however.

Hands can vary remarkably in shape, size, colouring and, of course, in the major lines. These display the difference between the potential and the actual in a subject. The need to make a living and to conform often overpowers a creative talent, for instance. You are bound to find many people who have been altered by the realities of social pressures.

It is sobering to note that the left hand is often clearer and cleaner than the right, illustrating the degree of repression of the natural, intuitive and erotic self by our society.

In the course of practice, I have come across notable exceptions to the 'read the right hand' rule. These exceptions have been the lateral thinkers, the people whose right brains are dominant. In their cases, it was correct to read the left hand.

Experience is the only way you will learn to make fine distinctions. In the meanwhile, concentrate on the right hand, regarding the left as the potential.

READING THE LINES

Lines read literally, and should be examined for irregularities of any sort. It is useful to consider the lines as power cables on a grid. Very pale, faded lines are not very effective in carrying power. Thick, bright red lines may be all too efficient at energy-bearing, making the subject overactive, hypertense, and even violent.

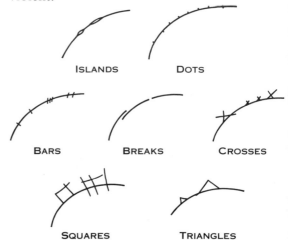

ISLANDS   DOTS

BARS   BREAKS   CROSSES

SQUARES   TRIANGLES

ISLANDS

Islands are generally a negative sign and represent split energy. They usually signify a difficult period, often of change.

As the Life Line represents the physical self, an island here often represents a period of ill-health. It can also show divided energy — perhaps someone who dislikes their work or their marriage.

An island on the Head Line can represent mental trauma, ranging from a breakdown to psychosis. It can also be a record of an actual injury to the head. In addition, it may indicate divided intellectual loyalties — perhaps the person is leading a way of life not fully accepted.

On the Heart Line it can mean divided emotional loyalties, hence the traditional interpretation of fickleness. It may also, accompanied by other signs in the hand, indicate cardiac disease.

DOTS

Dots are full-stops, and indicate a distinct interruption to the flow of energy. They are traditionally considered to be a sign of crisis. They certainly represent significant events.

On the Life Line dots mean a major shake-up: retrenchment, failure, demotion, and so on. On the Head Line they represent intellectual crisis. On the Heart Line the crisis is emotional.

BARS

Bars are blockages and often represent influences that arise outside the personality.

On the Life Line these are physical events — perhaps an actual barrier that must be faced and overcome.

On the Head Line they are a sign of mental blocks that reflect worry and/or lack of concentration.

On the Heart Line they may represent problems that arise within relationships, such as rejection and disillusionment.

BREAKS

Breaks are exactly that: the sign that a serious and major change to one's routine is at work; of energy quitting the old way and taking a new path. This new path may be negative or positive, and this may be assessed by examining the quality of the line which continues after the break.

On the Life Line breaks show travel, change of job or divorce. On the Head Line they represent a complete change in thinking, opinion or attitude.

On the Heart Line they are an indication of a clear break in affection (a 'broken heart'), emotional disillusionment or disappointment, and rejection.

CROSSES
Crosses on lines are traditionally considered to be very negative signs. Gloomy conclusions are often reached, involving death of loved ones, insanity, unrequited love and so forth.

SQUARES
Squares are a sign of protection and good fortune wherever they are found. They represent some environmental or personal factor that assists or protects the subject in most situations.

TRIANGLES
Triangles are positive marks. They indicate talent, creative ability and energy, and enhance the qualities of any line or mount on which they appear.

STARS
These are fairly uncommon signs that may indicate brilliance in a positive, well-formed character, or disaster in a negative hand, either enhancing or disrupting whatever line or mount on which they appear.

___

When studying the lines, do not be afraid to ask the subject questions about their past. A little judicious questioning can clarify and assist your reading a great deal. You will always run up against the character who will answer your questions with 'You're the palmist, you tell me.' My suggested reply to this is: 'When your doctor asks where it hurts, do you reply "Well you're the doctor, you tell me"?' Above all, don't be afraid of making mistakes!

READING THE MOUNTS

Novices often find the mounts difficult to locate and to access. It may help to consider the mounts as zones or areas on the palm, rather than look for bumps. Proper and accurate judgement of their size will only come with patience and experience.

There are several marks which commonly appear on the mounts:

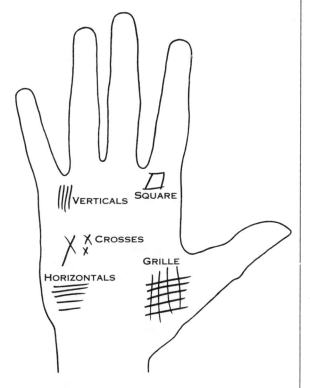

VERTICALS
Verticals are signs of vitality and energy in whatever area they are found.

HORIZONTALS
Horizontals are marks indicating stress, frustration and other problems wherever they are

found. They can also represent disruptive influences. For example, on Mount 6 (Venus), horizontals can show the interference and influence of close family and friends.

CROSSES

Crosses are usually considered negative signs, but there are at least three cases when crosses are a positive indication:

1 The 'happy marriage' cross, which lies in the area directly below finger 1, shows a personal disposition towards, and a talent for, fostering and nurturing relationships. Its absence, however, does not indicate the opposite.

2 The 'mystic cross', which is located between the Head and Heart lines, in the area beneath fingers 2 and 3. According to tradition, it indicates an interest in and a talent for occult (alternative) science.

3 The 'battle cross', which lies between the Fate and Life lines toward the base of the palm. some traditions claim it means that the subject will save life (or has already done so), while others say it shows a very quarrelsome disposition, with a love of battle. You may make up your own mind about this cross.

Elsewhere crosses represent trouble and worry, disappointment and unfavourable change. Here is a brief list of traditional readings:

Under finger 2: a sign of morbidity, perversion; an accident-prone personality, a gloomy pessimist.

Under finger 3: signals the frustrated artist; failure to translate artistic talent into material form.

Under finger 4: indicates dishonesty, exaggeration, lying and scheming.

On Mount 4 (Mars positive): marks a violent nature which resorts to force as a matter of policy.

On Mount 8 (Moon): shows a defect in imagination, or an over-active imagination leading to daydreaming, paranoia and withdrawal into a fantasy world; a person isolated from reality.

On Mount 6 (Venus): some traditions say it indicates an all-consuming love, others that it signals an unhappy marriage or love affair, or family in-fighting. Once again, you may make your own judgement.

Generally, crosses may be interpreted as disruptions to the coping process. They usually reflect a sensitive and delicate personality with a tendency to transform small and trivial issues into large problems.

GRILLES

Grilles show a scrambling of energy. They signal some form of malfunction where they occur, transforming the energy of the area, so that, for example, ambition becomes unhealthy obsession, love becomes selfish sensuality, executive skill becomes bullying, and so on. It often represents confusion because the energy of the mount involved becomes scattered and undirected.

SQUARES

These are positive signs of protection and preservation wherever they are found.

TIME

MEASUREMENT OF TIME ON THE MAJOR LINES

When considered as a diagnostic and psycho-analytic tool the hand is unique as it includes the fourth dimension of Time.

While the palm and the lines render the history of the subject accurately, the future is yet unformed, and consists of probabilities and possibilities. A competent palmist can read these probabilities, but it should be clearly understood that any predictions are only possibilities. Remember also, lines can change. If a hand shows distinct signs of future degeneration due to drug use or life-style, it is not necessarily an inevitable out-come. If a person changes his or her habits, the lines will change accordingly, reflecting the new future that will result. (See note on predicting the future on page 131.)

There are several ways to judge time on a line. Again, you will find that accuracy comes with practice.

Cheiro, a Victorian palmist, divided the major lines into ten equal parts and assigned seven years to each division. Here are two other useful methods I have found to be a fairly accurate guide:

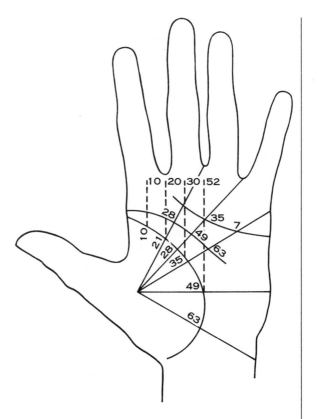

1 In the illustration above you will see straight lines drawn downwards from the bases of the fingers until they intersect the Life Line.

A straight line drawn down from the middle of finger 1 will intersect the Life Line at 10 years of age. A straight line drawn down from between fingers 1 and 2 will intersect the Life Line at age 20. A line from the middle of finger 2 will cross the Life Line at age 35. After that, the Life Line curves away. These readings are only generally accurate, with an error factor of plus or minus a year.

2 Simply measure the line in question and divide it in half, then into quarters. If you

127

judge the average life span to be 75 years, the halfway mark must be 37 or 38, and the quarters will mark the 19th and 56th years. You could then halve the quarters, giving you the 10th, 28th, 47th and 66th years.

You must take care to read the time-flow for each line in the right direction. The following illustration shows the direction of time-flow on the major lines.

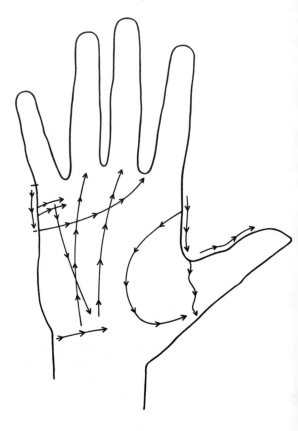

RINGS

There are some things you can observe before examining a subject's palm that will reveal a great deal about his or her character.

Rings (except for those worn on the third finger of the left hand — wedding rings) are considered an indication of difficulties within a person. The wearing of a ring tends to 'cut off' the qualities of the finger on which it is worn. The following is a brief list of the traditional meanings.

RIGHT HAND

Finger 1: If short, this person is troubled by an inferiority complex, and may over-compensate for the perceived lack by becoming a dominating, bullying tyrant.

If long, the person may be a chronic complainer who is never satisfied.

Finger 2: If short, this person is unstable and lacks self-discipline.

If long, the person is a critical, nagging complainer; a holier-than-thou troublemaker.

Finger 3: Whether short or long, the subject is experiencing frustration in their artistic or creative impulses; these may be caused by emotional ties, or a failure to create or exploit opportunities.

Finger 4: If short or long, the traditional reading is of dishonesty in business, and/or difficulties with relationships and sexual matters.

The thumb: Indicates one who is dissatisfied with sex in general, or with their current relationships.

LEFT HAND

Finger 1: If short, this is a sign of an inferiority complex compensated for by internal excess; over-achievement, over-indulgence in food, sex and alcohol.

If long, a person with a superiority complex who is troubled by their feelings and takes refuge in false modesty and self-depreciation.

Finger 2: If short, the lack of self-discipline within this person will be very disguised, yet visible through unreliability and instability.

If long, a very repressed, guilt-ridden person who suffers from inner turmoil and lack of self-respect.

Finger 3: Whether short or long, the wearing of more than one ring (e.g. a wedding band plus engagement, eternity, friendships rings) indicates emotional difficulties and problems in marriage or relationships.

Finger 4: Whether short or long, a sign of sexual and relationship problems, possibly 'inherited' from the parents.

The thumb: A sign of a person who experiences problems with sexual acts, and who may be frigid or impotent.

The actual size of the rings may also be significant. Small, unobtrusive rings signify a lesser influence than large, ornate rings.

USING THE READINGS

PREDICTING THE FUTURE

It is unwise to try to predict the future. Despite claims to the contrary, people persist in believing in palmistry, clairvoyance, and the like, and the danger of the self-fulfilling prophecy is always present.

Just announce at any party or social gathering that you read palms, and watch the people line up for their readings. Even skeptics seldom forget what you tell them.

Unfortunately, the type of palmistry which comes to the mind of most people is of the gypsy in a tea-room variety, wherein the hand is scanned briefly and is followed by an enigmatic pronouncement concerning the past and future. A stock of phrases general enough to be true for most people is used.

Palmistry deals with the person as they are at the time of the reading. Of course, the palm being a map of time as well as other dimensions, it is possible to see past and future possibilities, probabilities and likelihoods. It is not possible, however, to predict accidents and disappointments or lotto wins. These things, should they occur, will appear in the hand. One's history is traced with accuracy in the palm, but the future doesn't exist.

The fact is, the palm itself changes a great deal. Lines can appear and disappear overnight. What is on the palm doesn't change the person; rather, as people change, so do their palms.

Nevertheless, you will find that people generally believe that palmists are arcane mystics who can see into the future. Many people patronise palmists for that very reason.

However, the proper role of the palmist is to teach people about themselves, to give a gift of self-knowledge. In all likelihood the palmist will discern probabilities and trends regarding the personality and health of a subject in the course of a read, but it should always be stressed these are just possibilities, not inevitabilities, and that negative indications can be averted by taking appropriate steps.

NOTE FOR ASTROLOGERS

The connection of palmistry with astrology is obvious from the terminology they both use. They are similar in that they both attempt to create accurate, working analyses of people. Astrologers may use palmistry to confirm or clarify their own diagnoses. Certainly, many palmists use astrology to clear up points of palmistry.

For astrologers, palmistry can be a practical way to determine the strengths of aspects when they are ambiguous or obscure. A glance at the subject's hand will reveal the extent of the influence of any given planet.

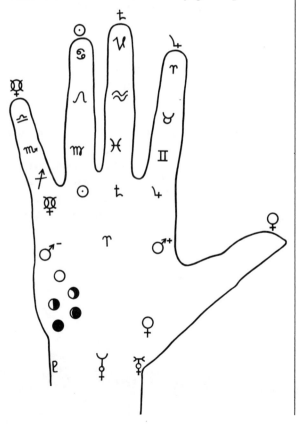

As it is interpretation, rather than mathematics, that lies at the base of the art of Astrology this cross-referencing, diagnostic tool could be valuable as a clarifier or confirmation.

See the diagram on page 133 for the astrological correspondences with the hand. The 3 phlanges of the 4 fingers give us the traditional 12 signs of the zodiac. The thumb signifies the ego, and is called by some traditions the 'finger of Venus'. It is the thumb, with its opposing grip to the fingers, that has allowed us to make so much technological progression. Without it, the use of tools would be impossible.

On the phlanges, there are four major marks to look for.

VERTICALS: These represent positive energy.

HORIZONTALS: These are bars and blocks of energy.

GRILLES: These indicate a scrambling of energy.

CROSSES: These signal that energy is being side-tracked.

In astrological terms, a vertical would be a good aspect, horizontals would be a retrograde sign, a cross a bad aspect, and a grille possibly neutral.

Reading Your Own Hand

The portable palmistry workshop is a biofeedback device. Just sit down, and answer each question as honestly as you are able. (This can be more difficult than it sounds!) You may well find yourself disagreeing with some of the answers. These are possibly aspects of yourself that you either do not recognize or do not wish to face up to, as such these are the areas that require the most attention.

In any case, the portable palmistry workshop offers you a unique opportunity for self-knowledge.

Naming the Demons

Each of us is a mixture of conflicting and complementary traits. If you have ever been puzzled by your own behaviour, or confused by your emotions, the Workshop can go a long way towards explaining and clarifying the way your intellectual and emotional energies work.

The fairy tale of Rumpelstiltskin will be familiar to many. Briefly, it describes how a young girl defeats a supernatural being (i.e. a subconscious aspect of herself) by discovering his name. The power of names is a common theme in mythology.

Now you too have the means to name your own personal demons, and it is astonishing just how much understanding, sympathy, and even love for ourselves we can achieve simply by becoming self-aware, by tapping directly into the deep well of our feelings and behaviour.

Your exploration of yourself can also reveal hidden or undeveloped talents, faults and limitations. This is the basis of self-knowledge. You can't change what you are not aware of.

So, name your demons, while not forgetting to celebrate and exploit your positive qualities. Remember, also, that your hand changes over time, and so it is possible to monitor yourself over a long period as lines change, appear and disappear, recording advances and changes in your makeup that result from experience.

The study of palmistry will in itself modify your hand as you add to your store of understanding of what Dr Johnson called the 'greatest study of mankind' — which is, of course, people.

THE ROLE OF REFLEXOLOGY

The principles of reflex massage have been known and used for centuries, particularly in China. These principles were rediscovered by Doctor William Fitzgerald in 1913, and introduced into Western medicine as 'zone therapy'. However, it has not been well accepted by mainstream medicine.

Reflexology is based on a similar theory to that of acupuncture: i.e. the body has a vital life force which circulates along pathways that encompass the entire body. These pathways have been extensively documented by Chinese medicine, but they do not match with the nervous, circulatory, lymphatic or any other system that Western medicine has so far been able to detect.

The pathways nevertheless exist, and their existence constitutes one of the major points of difference between the Western and Chinese theories of medicine.

These pathways can be tapped at more than 800 points on the body. The hands and feet, in particular, are rich in 'reflex buttons', which connect to all the major glands and organs. When these buttons or points are massaged or otherwise stimulated, they have a direct effect on the connecting organ. The stimulation of the points seems to have the effect of clearing the pathways so that the life energy can flow freely. (In Chinese theory, disease is often the result of blockages in the free flow of life energy through the channels.) The removal or easing of blockages assists the body to heal by allowing the normal healing processes to act without hindrance.

Regular massage can assist in alleviating and relieving both chronic and acute conditions. It can even be self-administered. One should not underestimate the healing aspects of simply holding and gently massaging some-one's hand.

A properly conducted examination of a hand by a student of palmistry can constitute a reflexology massage. As you feel and squeeze the hands, seeking out the hollows (weaknesses) and testing the bulges (strengths), a feeling of relaxation and well-being in the subject should become evident. This is useful, as a palm-reading can be a mild crisis for some people, provoking anxiety. They might be afraid that you will find some terrible doom to sour their future. In any case, the offering of the hands palm up is the attitude of submission and surrender, which in itself could make the subject feel vulnerable.

If you happen to locate any tender or painful spots, advise the subject to massage these points themselves later, as they probably represent some physical problem present in the body.

A full reflexology massage is a loving and healing gift to give anyone. Use a light oil and sit facing the subject as though for a palm reading. You must work each hand in turn, completing each step on both hands before moving on to the next step. Here are the steps:

1 Work your thumbs over each palm in a firm, circular motion.

2 Work the hollows between the tendons on the back of the hands. These are rich in acupressure points, and 'open' the whole hand. Work from the wrist towards the fingers.

3 Massage the webbing between the fingers. These are considered 'toxic' points, where tension may accumulate.

4 Now, take each finger in turn (including the thumb) and
   (a) tug it firmly,
   (b) gently twist it back and forth,
   (c) press hard on the tip,
   (d) work the spaces between the joints, concentrating on the sides of the fingers.
5 Lace your fingers with the subject's and stretch the fingers backwards.
6 Stretch the thumbs back (but don't force them) towards the wrist several times.
7 Flex and fold the palm in on itself, using pressure on the sides of the hand.
8 Have the subject flap and wave the hands about in a loosening motion.
9 Use your fist to press all over the palm, then pound it gently, using the right fist and supporting with the left.
10 Give a brisk all-over rub.

Use this as a basic technique and do not hesitate to add your own variations. A great deal of variety is possible. Just do what feels right and loving.

NOTE FOR PARENTS

Palmistry is an excellent way to evaluate and understand your child's character. From the moment of birth, a wealth of information can be gleaned from your baby's hand. The three major lines are immediately present in the hands of babies. This shows that the three basic energies of the human animal are present — physical, emotional and intellectual.

The hand of a child is very changeable. It can be interesting to take regular prints (or photocopies) of a growing hand and see how the lines and mounts reflect the emerging personality.

Changes in the lines can be dramatic: the emotional turmoil of puberty often creates much disruption in the form of islands and dots on the Head and Heart lines. Even more interesting, the early segments of the major lines will reflect your influence as a parent on the child.

The greatest benefit is, of course, your own increased perception and appreciation of your child's character. Their talents, intelligence and faults can all be detected and evaluated from an early age. The sensitive, artistic child can be appropriately nurtured and encouraged; the intelligent or creative child can be given direction; and the high-energy, sports minded type can be offered suitable outlets for that energy.

A general check on health can also be maintained by palmistry. Keep an eye out for stress marks on fingers during crucial periods such as examinations, starting new schools, and so on.

A sensitive familiarity with your children's hands (not to mention your spouse's) will assist both them and yourself.

NOTE FOR PERSONNEL MANAGERS

The task of the personnel manager might be fairly and simply stated as finding the right person for the right job. In the past twenty years a great number of psychological tests have developed to test job applicants for qualities such as leadership, maths skills, motivation, intelligence and much else.

The validity of many tests is often questionable. It is always possible to fake answers and manipulate results. Whatever the case, there are weaknesses inherent in many of the assumptions made by such tests. References are only partially helpful in assessing a candidate for a position, and often tell little of enduring traits of the potential employee. Many people are excellent at interviews, yet turn out to perform poorly on the job. Then again, someone who may be ideal for a position could be nervous at interviews and fail to impress.

Employers sometimes refer potential workers to graphologists, others turn to astrologers. These methods are both useful — graphology in particular — but the majority of appointments seem to occur on the basis of references and tests.

As the hand is an unbiased map of one's abilities, talents and potential, modern palmistry would be an ideal tool for assessing these characteristics. Desired and undesired qualities can be detected at a glance, with no possibility of deception. The palm cannot lie.

Are you looking for a manager? If so, the applicant's hand will tell you if the requisite qualities — organisational skill, honesty, reliability — are there. Are you seeking a supervisor with some creative flair, or one who is solid and capable of getting the job done as specified? Do you need a worker with a flair for figures, or one who is subtle and sensitive with clients? Is a worker honest? Is he or she ambitious, aggressive, happy to be in a subordinate position?

Palmistry can provide the answers to these decisions. For example, if you are seeking an executive, have a good look at the index finger (finger 1). Is it longer than the ring finger (finger 3)? If it is, you have a naturally dominant type, who is unsuited by temperament to a subordinate position, especially where there is no scope for advancement. If the index finger is curved, so that it leans toward the other fingers, it is a sign that the applicant has a problem with self-confidence, and doubts his or her ability.

Now look at the bottom phlange of the index finger. Is it strongly marked with vertical lines? If so, the person has good organisational skills and is capable of inspiring staff. If there are also bar lines or a grille, then there exists a strong tendency toward manipulation, perhaps a penchant for office politics, which may or may not suit you as an employer.

Now look at the Head Line. If it is clean, clear and very straight, you have a logical type who will excel at figures, but may be poor at handling problems requiring sensitivity or creative flair. If you need an executive who is imaginative, sympathetic and inventive, then look for a curved head line.

Does the job involve selling? Then look for strong vertical lines on the bottom phlange of the little finger (finger 4). If there are bar lines in the area, you have before you a convincing liar.

Do you need a manager who is both practical and reliable, who will stick to the job stubbornly and single-mindedly? Then find an Earth hand, with a good Head Line and a strong Fate Line. Such a person can be counted on to be rather authoritative, though regrettably insensitive in the area of employer/employee relationships. He or she does not suffer fools gladly, and will have great difficulty understanding personal problems among the staff. On the other hand, a manager with a Water hand would be ideal for positions requiring tact and sensitivity.

Positions requiring flexibility, enthusiasm and good staff motivational skills would best suit the Fire hand, while the job needing an analytical, systematic approach would best be filled by an Air hand.

Using such simple guidelines, palmistry can be a useful cross-reference to established procedures, an alternative method of avoiding the costly misplacement of round pegs in square holes.

Any readers interested in this method of personnel evaluation are welcome to contact the author, c/o the publisher.

NOTE FOR LOVERS AND MARRIAGE GUIDANCE COUNSELLORS

The gentle application of palmistry to the area of emotional relationships can greatly aid understanding between the parties involved. The exploration of character through the palm will help people to understand themselves and their partner, and areas of conflict and compatibility can be thoroughly explored.

In the palm, you will easily discover the really major differences that tend to cause conflict in relationships. Some are readily apparent: a strong sex drive versus a low sex drive, the security-conscious versus the rolling stone, the party-goer versus the stay-at-home type. Perhaps the partners are both dominant types, which can cause conflicts as each struggles to settle a pecking order.

There are many other differences, greater and lesser, that can escalate into disharmony and separation. You can also see how individual inner conflicts reflect in a relationship.

For the marriage guidance counsellor, a mutual reading is a good idea: a two-hour session, which can be formalised by such techniques as the use of a blackboard divided into three segments — two devoted to each individual, and one to their aspect as a couple. The idea is to list the main negative and positive qualities of each partner so that compatibilities and differences become obvious.

Each point should be discussed before committing it to writing. This segment of the session can be very lively due to palmistry's startling accuracy. This truthfulness is palmistry's great strength. Bluster and denial cease to be of much use when one is confronted with irrefutable truth.

Your attitude as a palmist is most important. You must be disinterested and objective, with no desire to sway anyone to any particular point of view, only to relate truthfully what you find in the hand.

The ability to accept the findings can be a measure of the subject's self-knowledge. A good guidance session is a direct confrontation with the truth. Individuals are brought face-to-face with their inner personalities, down to their deepest motivations.

The bottom line in fathoming human relationships is that love can only be based on mutual recognition and understanding.

However, it need not be too serious. Palmistry can be a party game or a lover's game, a voyage of mutual discovery, a way of sizing someone up before things get too serious. Such understanding can lead to the enhancement of a love match — or the opposite, an appreciation of why love cannot last. Either way, both parties will be better off.

THE ESOTERICA

There are many systems of palmistry. The Indians and the Chinese, for instance, have systems which seem to be quite different from Western palmistry. There is evidence that the Egyptians and the Greeks also used palmistry.

The main thing all systems hold in common is the direct relationship between humanity and the cosmos, and, since the hand is a map of the person, it could also be said that the hand is a map of the universe.

Each system of palmistry is based on varying cosmologies and belief systems. Take Indian palmistry as an example. It is probably trite to attempt to define the complexities and richness of Indian theology in just a few lines, but their philosophy tends towards theories of predestination: that people, driven by karma, lead fated lives. This idea of inevitability gives to Indian palmistry an unacceptable (from the New Age Palmistry viewpoint) degree of insistence on future prediction.

Of course, the Indian system of palmistry works very well for Indians. It has evolved to fit their rigid caste system, their religiously defined social structure. In traditional rural villages the organisation of the four major castes — the priests, the warriors, the merchants, the untouchables — can be seen functioning today as it has for 2000 years. It may be seen that the life of the individual is fated in such a rigid and stratified society. The sons of priests grow up to be priests and marry the daughters of priests. Marriage out of caste doesn't, as a rule, occur. Likewise, many occupations are inherited.

Social mobility is more common in Western society, and it is this that invalidates Indian systems of palmistry for the New Age palmist. Cultural and philosophical differences also render Chinese palmistry unsuitable, even though there are many points of similarity and correspondence.

NEW AGE PSYCHIC REFLEXOLOGY CHART

The illustration on the right attempts to display the relationship between the cosmos, represented by traditional astrological signs and meanings, and the microcosmos, each individual.

It shows the important division of the hand into four quarters: the conscious intellectual self, the subconscious intellectual self, the conscious emotional self, and the subconscious emotional self. It is possible to make a quick assessment of a subject simply by observing whether there is a concentration of marks or lines in any one quarter.

The strengths and weaknesses of a particular zone may be seen by noting the four common signs found in the palm: *verticals,* representing the positive flow of natural energy; *horizontals,* indicating stress and interruptions to the free flow of energy; *grilles,* which scramble and confuse energy; and *crosses,* which can either accentuate or divert energy.

Areas clear of markings signal positive potential energy.

The illustration is also useful as a psychic reflexology chart.

PSYCHOLOGICAL REFLEXOLOGY CHART OF THE HUMAN HAND

These zones show the relationships between the cosmos and microcosmos. The person's strengths and weaknesses in each zone may be discerned by seeking marks in any zone. There are 5 common signs:

VERTICALS	Positive flow of natural energy
BARS	Stress and breaks in flow of energy and confuses the flow of natural energy
SCRAMBLES	The flow of natural energy
CROSSES	Can accentuate or divert energy
CLEAR AREA	Positive potential energy

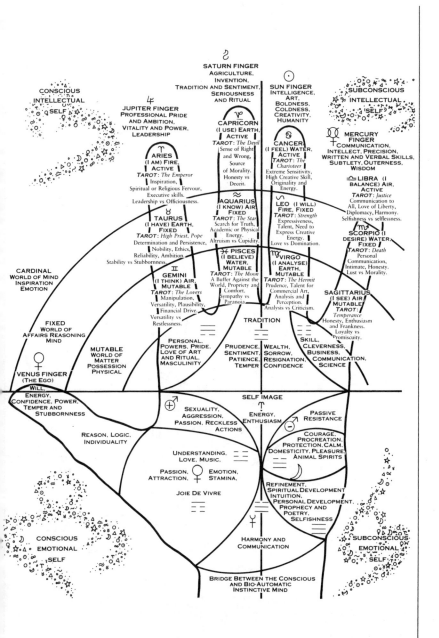

THE CHINESE HAND

This consists of a symbolic graphic, taken from the *I Ching*, and rendered onto the hand.

Students of the *I Ching* may spend hours finding areas of intriguing correspondence with the traditional Western layouts of the hand. The interesting aspect is the number of points of agreement between the oriental and occidental systems, for despite the fact that they depart on most points, they ultimately come to very similar conclusions.

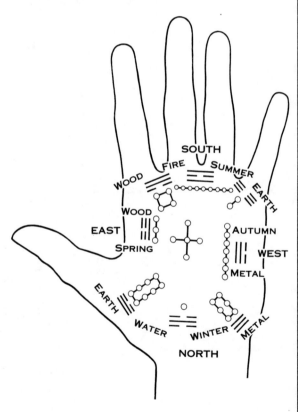

Here is a brief list of the qualities of the eight mounts as defined by the *I Ching*.

Mount 1 (Jupiter/Saturn): Wind, wood, South-east, the eldest daughter, the thigh, early Summer, mid-morning, flexibility, gentleness and gradual, penetrating influence.

Mount 2 (Saturn/Apollo): Fire (sun, lightning), South, the middle daughter, the eye, mid-Summer, noon, brightness, elegance, intelligence and illumination.

Mount 3 (Apollo/Mercury): Earth, South-west, the mother, the belly, early Autumn, night, capaciousness, submission, yielding, darkness, responsive, receptivity and nourishment.

Mount 4 (Mars positive): Thunder, East, the eldest son, the foot, Spring, early morning, arousal, activity, movement and exciting power.

Mount 5 (Mars negative/Upper Luna): Water (a lake or a marsh), West, the youngest daughter, the mouth, late Autumn, twilight, satisfaction, fullness, complacency and pleasure.

Mount 6 (Venus): Mountain, North-east, the youngest son, the hand, late Winter, dawn, tranquillity, resting, being calm, patience, waiting and immovability.

Mount 7 (Neptune): Water (rain and clouds), North, the middle son, the ear, mid-winter, midnight, difficulty, danger and anxiety.

Mount 8 (Moon): Heaven, East, the father, the head, early Winter, daytime, creativity, strength and untiring power.

ONE TRADITIONAL HAND

The following is a description of the ideal progression of a life, and is derived from a mediaeval manuscript.

Life is a cyclic process: all that exists goes through an inevitable cycle of birth, growth, maturity, decay and death, and this is reflected in the hand.

From birth to puberty is our period of growth. During this time we are conditioned to the basic attitudes and values that shape our lives. Further growth occurs during our teen years (the age of reason), when further education takes place.

Maturity comes as we begin to apply ourselves to the creation of a lifestyle. Acquired skills are practised and perfected.

Gradually, growth ends and we are mature. The achievement of maturity should usher in a long period of peace and contentment. The 'ideal' pattern for life is clear — birth, education, work, peace and fulfilment.

Of course, the time-spans of these processes vary greatly in each individual. Some people remain longer in one stage or another, while others move rapidly through the early stages of their development to arrive at fulfilment and peace. What stage are *you* in?

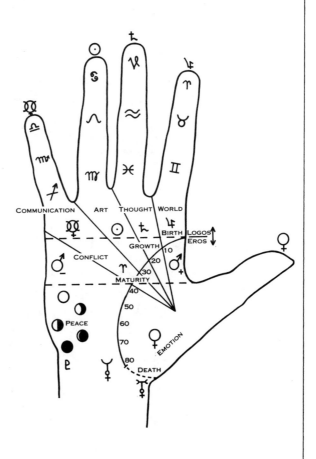

THE WICCAN HAND

The extremely ancient belief-system known as wicca divides the person into seven layers (or levels) inside two bodies (or forms). The seven layers relate to planets. The two forms represent the perishable personality and the imperishable (or eternal) part of the self.

THE PERISHABLE PERSONA

1 *Basal:* This is the entire hand and particularly the Mount of the Moon, and is symbolised by the Earth.
2 *Lower astral:* This contains instinct, passion and desire, and is symbolised by Mars.

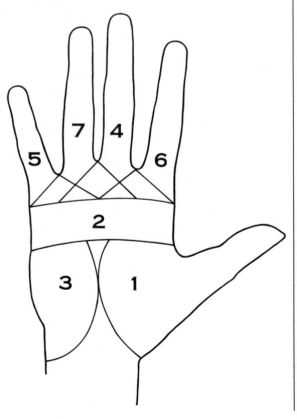

3 *Upper astral:* This contains abstract emotion and idealism, and is ruled by Venus.
4 *Lower mental:* This is the 'concrete mind', ruled by Saturn.

THE IMPERISHABLE PERSONA
5 *Upper mental:* Ruled by Mercury,
6 *Upper spiritual:* Ruled by Jupiter,
7 *Upper spiritual:* Ruled by the Sun (Apollo).

These three eternal areas represent creative power and energy.

FURTHER READING

Here is a brief list of some of the titles consulted:

Elizabeth Brenner, *The Hand Book* (1980), Bay Books, Sydney.

Cheiro, *Language of The Hand* (1967), Corgi, London.

Andrew Fitzherbert, *Hand Psychology* (1986), Angus & Robertson, Sydney.

C. de St Germain, *The Practice of Palmistry* (1973), Newcastle Publications, U.S.A.

Katherine St Hill, *Grammar of Palmistry* (1973), Sugar Publications, New Delhi.

Peter West, *Lifelines* (1973), Piper Press, New Delhi.

OTHER NATURAL HEALTH TITLES FROM LOTHIAN

Judy Jacka
A–Z OF NATURAL THERAPIES

Here is a clear and simple reference for anyone seeking information on how natural therapies deal with a wide variety of illness, and how professional therapists work.

Judy Jacka discusses symptoms, causes, treatments and case histories to encourage an understanding of a healthy body.

Also by Judy Jacka
FRONTIERS OF NATURAL THERAPIES

Among the traditional therapies, acupuncture, chiropractic, herbal medicine, homoeopathy, meditation and Tai Chi are but a few of the many therapies now widely practised in the Western world. Added to them are exciting developments in our understanding of the energy fields which are related to bio-energetic medicine, vega-testing and psychosomatics. These new approaches to health all have the common goal of seeking to promote a good life-style and to use natural medicines and methods to improve health. This book examines the principles and practice behind all natural therapies and wherever possible provides a scientific framework for the concepts.

DOROTHY HALL'S HERBAL MEDICINE
This is the long awaited herbal by Dorothy
Hall, natural therapist and herbalist
extraordinary. She writes as only she can —
reflecting her years of research, her familiarity
with the plants, her clinical knowledge of the
physiological and other effects of herbal
treatments, and her unique perceptions and
understanding of the human character.

Dorothy Hall's is a new and fresh approach to
herbal medicine, discussing personality
analysis through herbs and demonstrating
how particular person-pictures can be built
up by looking at the person's needs for
particular herbs.

John Vriend
EYES TALK
THROUGH IRIDOLOGY TO BETTER
HEALTH
Your brain is like a computer; your eyes are
the screens. They function as a health warning
system and tell you what is happening
elsewhere in your body.

John Vriend is an experienced iridologist and
nutritional consultant and in this book he
explains the anatomy of the eye; the iridology
chart; how to examine the iris; parts of the
body; bodily systems and places iridology in
the broader context of personal health care
with herbal and nutritional advice and simple
remedies.